Letters
from
Korean
History

Notes on the English translation

Korean personal names, place names, proper nouns and common nouns have been transliterated according to the Revised Romanization of Korean system, introduced by the South Korean government in 2000. The only exceptions are names that are widely recognized in other forms, such as Syngman Rhee (Lee Seungman) or Kim Ilsung (Kim Ilseong). Two of the most common Korean surnames, Kim and Park, have been left in their conventional forms, rather than Gim and Bak (which would be their spellings according to the Revised Romanization system). The surname Lee, meanwhile, is transliterated as Yi before 1945, in accordance with convention (for example, Yi Seonggye), and then in the more modern form of Lee after 1945, taking Korean liberation as a somewhat arbitrary dividing line. Surnames are listed before first names, in the Korean style, with the singular, Americanized exception of Syngman Rhee.

The ages of individuals are listed in accordance with the original Korean text of *Letters from Korean History*, which naturally follows the Korean convention for age calculation. This means that figures given are generally one year higher than what would be considered the corresponding "Western" age.

Letters from Korean History

4

From late Joseon to the Daehan Empire

Park Eunbong

CUM LIBRO 책과함께

History in Northeast Asia is like a minefield. Riddled with unresolved issues, controversies, disputed territory and conflicting ideologies, it often breeds acrimony among governments and peoples in the region. Within many countries, too, blind nationalism, political bias and censorship constantly threaten to distort the picture painted by historians of their country's past and, by extension, present. Creating a balanced narrative in the midst of such tension and conflicting perspectives is no easy task. But that is what Park Eunbong appears to have done in *Letters from Korean History*.

Offering children and young readers an unbiased version of their past is one of the kindest and most responsible ways of helping them grow into broad-minded citizens, capable of sustaining peace and cooperation in a region - and world - that grows more interconnected every year but still bears unhealed historical scars and bruises. In Korea, such a history also offers context that can put the country's current state of division - only sixty-seven years old as of 2015 - into wider perspective.

Making any Korean book accessible to readers of English through translation is a privilege. The same goes for *Letters from Korean History*. In a series of letters addressed to a young reader overseas, the author adopts a conversational style of writing that conveys the ups and downs, ins and outs of Korean history with ease. But while the language is highly accessible, the content is never rendered simplistic or patronizing, and issues that lose some other historians in a fog of

nationalism are navigated by Park with the kind of healthy detachment and clarity that inspires confidence in the reader.

Progressing from the stones and bones of prehistory all the way to the turbulent twentieth century in the course of five volumes, *Letters from Korean History* can be browsed as a reference text or plowed through from beginning to end. As with most histories that cover such a long period, the density of information increases as the narrative approaches the present. The relatively recent Joseon period, for example, accounts for two of the five volumes (III and IV), rich as it is in events and meticulously recorded historical data.

Letters from Korean History has been a great success in its native country among Korean readers. I hope that this translation will now be of help to ethnic Koreans overseas, others interested in Korea or history in general, Koreans looking to study history and English at the same time, and anybody else who believes that exploring the past is a good way to try and make sense of the confusing, flawed and wonderful present.

Ben Jackson
May, 2016

To readers of 'Letters from Korean History'

Letters from Korean History is a series of some seventy letters covering a period that stretches from prehistory to the present. Unlike most introductions to Korean history, it takes a theme-based approach: each theme functions as a window onto a particular period. The use of several different windows offering various perspectives onto the same period is meant to help the reader form her or his own more complete picture of that part of history. For example, "Buddhism, key to the culture of the Three Kingdoms" and "Silla, land of the bone-rank system," two letters in Volume I, offer two different ways of understanding Silla history: a religious perspective via Buddhism; and a social caste-based perspective by way of the bone-rank system. My hope is that, after reading both letters and exploring these two separate approaches, readers will come closer to gaining a comprehensive understanding of Silla. The more diverse the windows opened, the more helpful this should be in the forming of a complete image.

Letters from Korean History places equal emphasis on aspects such as culture, everyday life, society and social segments with habitually low historical profiles, such as women and children. This is an important difference to conventional introductory histories, which naturally tend towards narratives centered on ruling classes by prioritizing political history.

I have also attempted to portray Korean history not as that of a single nation in isolation but as part of world history as a whole, and to adopt a perspective that places humans as just one species in the universe and nature. This is why the first letter begins not with prehistory on the Korean Peninsula but with the birth of the human race on Earth. The connection with world history is maintained

throughout the five volumes, in which Korea's interactions, relationships and points of comparison with the rest of the world are constantly explored.

The single most distinct aspect of *Letters from Korean History* is that, unlike most general histories, which make passing references to characters and dates, it depicts Korea's past through a series of engaging stories. It is my hope that these will help readers feel like direct witnesses to historical scenes as they unfold. All content is based on historical materials, either in their original form or adapted without distortion. Sources include key texts such as *Samguk sagi* ("History of the Three Kingdoms"), *Samguk yusa* ("Memorabilia of the Three Kingdoms"), *Goryeosa* ("History of Goryeo") and *Joseon wangjo sillok* ("Royal Annals of the Joseon Dynasty"), as well as a variety of literary anthologies, letters, journals and epigraphs.

The English version of *Letters from Korean History* is published for young readers overseas who are curious about Korea and its people, and for young Korean readers keen to learn more about their own history while improving their language skills as global citizens. I hope that readers will not feel obliged to start at the beginning of Volume I and plow all the way through; rather, each letter contains a historical episode in its own right, and can be chosen and read according to the reader's particular area of interest. The text is complemented by plenty of photos and illustrations, giving a more vivid sense of history - reading the captions that accompany these should enhance the sense of historical exploration.

I very much hope that this book will become a useful source of guidance for young readers, wherever they may be.

Park Eunbong

May, 2016

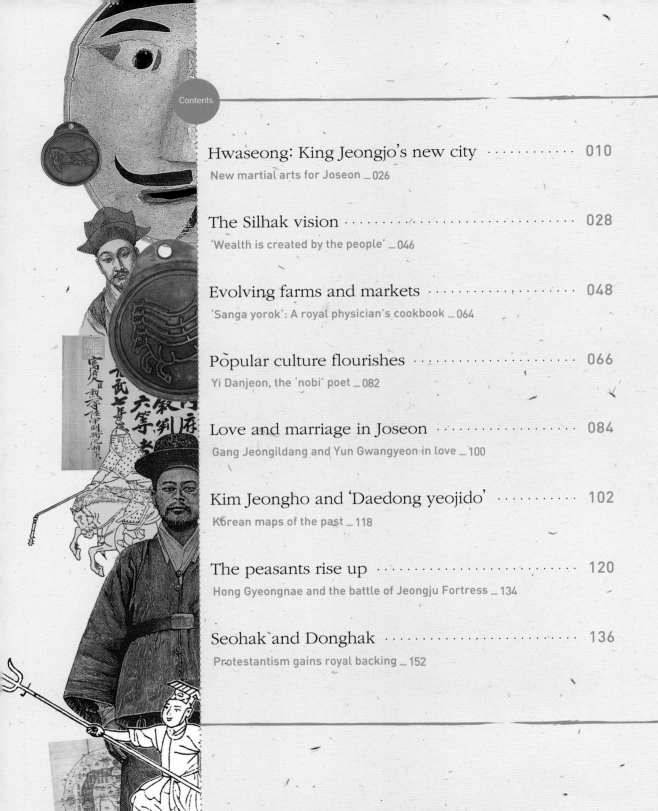

Contents

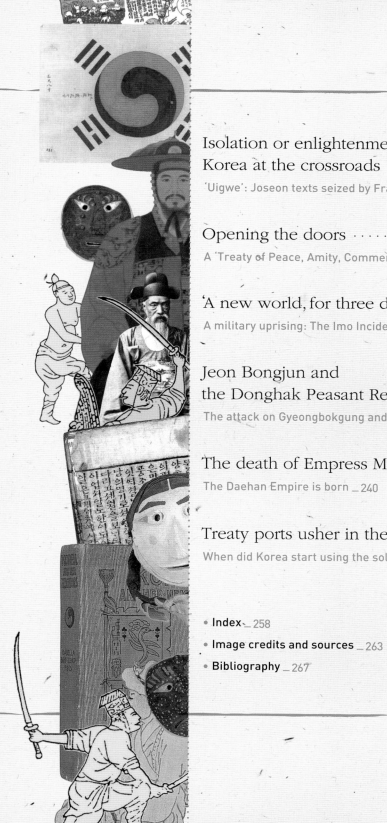

CHAPTER 1

Hwaseong: King Jeongjo's new city

After eradicating the factionalism that had led to the death of his father, he would soar up into the sky and, like a moon shining light down on all the rivers and streams of the land, rule in an absolute yet fair and impartial manner that would ensure a good life for his people. Hwaseong would be the seat of this future government. This should give you some idea of why the new city meant so much to the king.

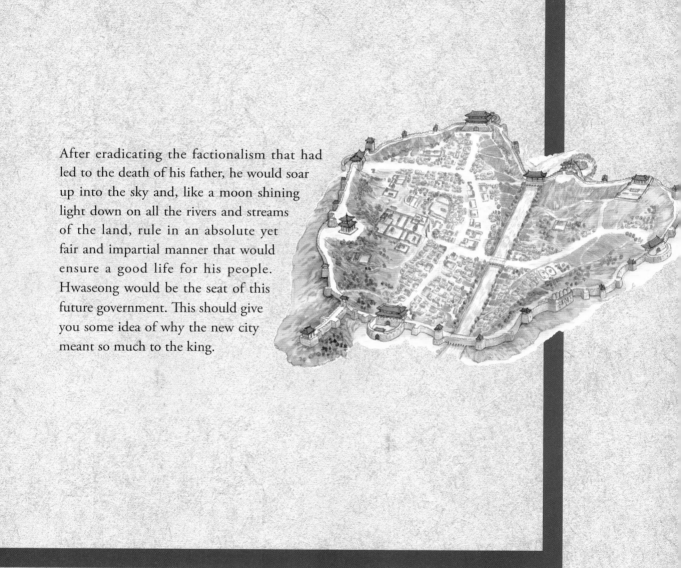

| T I M E | L I N E |

1776
Joseon period
Jeongjo takes throne;
builds Gyujanggak

1780
Park Jiwon travels to Qing;
writes 'Yeolha ilgi'

1791
'Keumnanjeongwon'
abolished except
for Yuguijeon

Have you ever been to Hwaseong Fortress? It stands in what is now the city of Suwon in Gyeonggi-do Province.

Jeongjo, the twenty-second king of Joseon, devoted himself to building Hwaseong. The new city was smaller than Hanyang, but its location, south of the capital, made it a powerful defensive presence. The state-of-the-art fortress wall that ran around it was a masterpiece, built using the very latest science and technology. It was not only strong, but beautiful.

"Why make a fortress look good if its function is to withstand fierce enemy attacks?" asked one of Jeongjo's ministers.

"So it defeats the enemy with its beauty," the king replied.

Among the many monarchs of Joseon, Jeongjo was the most erudite and intelligent. And he had a special reason for building Hwaseong.

In order to understand the king's motives, let's take a look at the grand eight-day procession he made from Hanyang to the new city in 1795.

1834	1836	1861	1862
Yeom Gyedal performs *'pansori'* for King Heonjong	Yun Gwangyeon publishes wife's collected works in *'Jeongildang yugo'*	Kim Jeongho completes *'Daedong yeojido'*	Peasant uprising in Jinju

Jeongjo rose early on the day the procession to Hwaseong was to begin. The journey was extremely important to him: he had decided to celebrate his mother's sixtieth birthday at the tomb of his father, Crown Prince Sado.

Hopefully you will recall the story of Sado, which I mentioned in a previous letter. Caught in the vicious currents of factionalism in the royal court, the crown prince was shut in a rice chest and left to die. Jeongjo was just eleven years old at the time, but he never stopped thinking of his father in all the years afterwards. He considered Sado's death to have been unjust, and it had made him resolve to uproot once and for all the factionalism that had led to such a terrible event.

Gyeongmogung Shrine
Built by King Jeongjo in memory of his late father, Prince Sado, this shrine originally stood in a garden attached to Changgyeonggung Palace. The shrine is now gone, replaced by Seoul National University Hospital, leaving only a few steps and a gate as traces of its former existence. This photo, taken before the Korean War, shows part of the shrine.

Today's procession to Hwaseong served as an unmistakable statement of this resolve. Ostensibly, it was being billed as a birthday celebration, but its actual purpose was twofold: to console the late Sado's aggrieved spirit, and to warn members of the Noron faction, whose machinations had led to the prince's untimely death, that his son was not somebody to be messed with.

The procession also offered a way for Jeongjo to place trust in his loyal followers and to let the people know just how dignified their king was. Starting on the ninth day of the second February, a leap month (see page 257), in 1795, (the year *eulmyo* according to the Joseon calendar) and lasting for eight days, the event unfolded as follows.

From Hanyang to Hwaseong in eight days

Jeongjo hurriedly got dressed and made his way outside. Departure time for the procession was *myosi* ("rabbit o' clock"; from five to seven in the morning). After saying goodbye to Jeongsun, his step-grandmother, he came out of Changdeokgung Palace through Donhwamun, the main gate, and waited. When his mother, Lady Hyegyeong, finally emerged from the palace in her palanquin, the procession began.

Jeongjo chose to ride on horseback rather than in a palanquin. He must have looked like a powerful general,

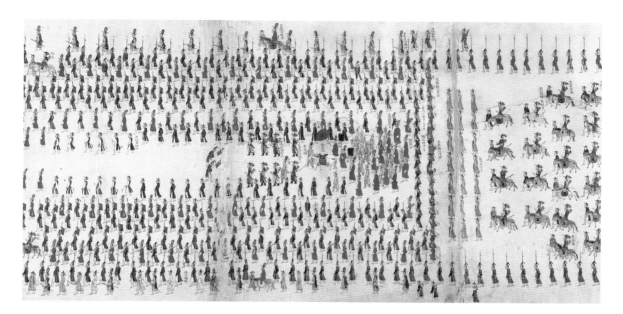

sitting astride his horse in his military uniform. 1,779 people and 779 horses took part in the procession itself, but when you count those who had already traveled to Hwaseong in advance and those who had turned out along the route to wait for it to pass, the number rises to something like 6,000.

Preparation for the procession was meticulous. A new road was built from Hanyang to Hwaseong—known today as the Siheung Road—and lined with rest areas, places to stay the night, and even temporary buildings for catering.

The procession left Hanyang through Sungnyemun, the city's main southern gate, passed through the area where Seoul Station stands today, and reached Yongsan. From there, anyone on the way to Hwaseong had to cross the Hangang River. How did they do this in the days when there was no bridge?

The Hwaseong Procession
Jeongjo spent much time preparing for the procession to Hwaseong. It was both a celebration of his mother's sixtieth birthday and an opportunity to demonstrate his own dignity.

Roads to Hwaseong
This map shows the route taken by Jeongjo on his way from Changdeokgung Palace to Hwaseong. This time, he traveled along the newly-built road Siheung Road, shown here on the left, instead of the old road, which runs via Gwacheon, on the right.

It was here that the most magnificent scene of the whole procession unfolded: the crossing of a temporary pontoon bridge, laid over a series of boats moored side by side in a line stretching across the river.

This was not the first pontoon bridge to span the Hangang. This time, however, Jeongjo and his ministers had made a detailed plan to build one as cheaply and quickly as possible. After lining up thirty-six merchant boats on the river, they laid a temporary road of wooden planks on top. It took just eleven days to complete the structure, which was located roughly half-way between today's Hangangdaegyo and Hangangcheolgyo bridges.

The sight of Lady Hyegyeong's palanquin, Jeongjo on his horse, and row upon row of officials and soldiers as the procession slowly crossed the pontoon bridge, its colored banners flapping in the wind, was nothing short of spectacular. Both banks of the river were crammed with onlookers eager to catch a glimpse. Jeongjo, keen to build himself a dignified image among his people, had given explicit orders that they be allowed to come close and watch the grand procession.

The procession crossed the river without mishap, crested the hill at Jangseungbaegi, and headed for Siheung. Soon, the sun began to set. At Siheung, there was a *haenggung*—a provincial palace reserved for traveling monarchs—where the king and his retinue were to stay the night. This, too, had been newly built for the procession. When they arrived, Jeongjo had dinner served.

"What a happy day this has been!" he said to his ministers. "The weather was fine and my mother is in good health. This meal is a gift from her - enjoy it!"

Once the king and his retinue had passed the night in Siheung, the procession resumed early the next morning. It crossed Manangyo Bridge, passed through Anyangcham (near the site of today's Anyang subway station) and stopped for lunch at Sageuncham-haenggung Temporary Palace. Just then, it began to rain, and the procession gathered pace.

Finally, they reached Janganmun, the northern gate of Hwaseong. If you pass through Janganmun, head south towards Paldalmun, then turn right, you reach Hwaseonghaenggung Temporary Palace. Here, the king escorted his mother to a building called Jangnakdang, then sat down for dinner. The procession had covered a distance of 63 *ri* (a Joseon unit of distance measurement) from Changdeokgung to Hwaseong.

The next morning, a four-day celebration

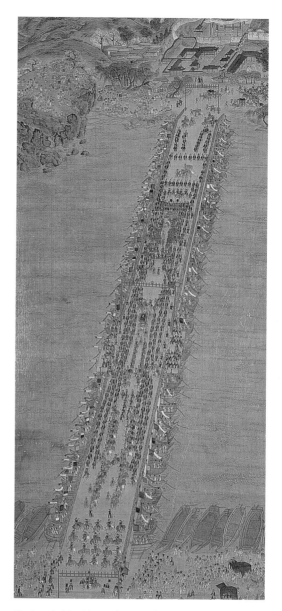

Pontoon bridge *Hongsalmun*, red gates with rows of spikes across the top, were placed to mark the two ends and the center of the bridge. This painting shows the procession returning from Hwaseong to Hanyang. At the top of the picture is the southern bank of the Hangang; at the bottom is the northern side. Can you see Lady Hyegyeong's palanquin passing beneath one of the *hongsalmun*? Behind her is Jeongjo, surrounded by his military guards.
−National Palace Museum of Korea

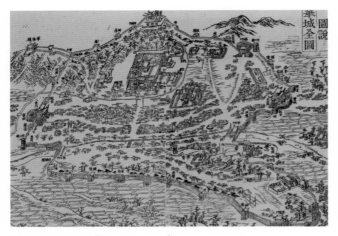

'Hwaseong jeondo' ('Complete Map of Hwaseong')
Produced in 1796, the year after Jeongjo's procession, this map shows Hwaseong in its entirety. The fortress city is full of houses and surrounded by rice paddies.
– Kyujanggak Institute for Korean Studies

comprising various events began. A state examination was held for local Confucian scholars and warriors, while a memorial service was held at Crown Prince Sado's tomb, Hyeollyungwon. Two military training exercises were held, one during the day and one at night, in the presence of the king. Lady Hong's birthday party was followed by a banquet to which 384 elderly local people were invited. Free rice and salt were handed out to widows, widowers, orphans, childless elderly people, and the poor.

On the fifteenth day of the second February, the four-day celebration ended and the procession set off once again for Hanyang, following the same route back. When it had crossed Jinmokjeonggyo Bridge, it reached Mireukhyeon, a hill that separates what are now the cities of Suwon and Uiwang. This is the last point on the way back to the capital from which Hwaseong and Hyeollyungwon can be seen. Jeongjo stopped his horse.

"Whenever I reach Mireukhyeon, I don't want to leave. I stop my horse and spend quite a while gazing back to the south. Sometimes, I find myself dismounting and lingering even longer. See that round stone up there? Have it named 'Jiji.' And put a sign at the foot of Mireukhyeon saying 'Jijidae'."

"Jiji" means "slowly, slowly." Jeongjo chose this name to express the feeling that overcame him every time he reached this spot and slowed down, reluctant to leave the place where his beloved father was buried.

Jijidae stele
Inside this wooden pavilion is a stele that tells the story of Jijidae. The name is carved in Chinese characters on the steps leading up to the building.

❗ 'Wonhaeng eulmyo jeongni uigwe'

'Wonhaeng eulmyo jeongni uigwe'
Uigwe include depictions of key scenes from state events. Known as *banchado*, these paintings are striking for their precise detail and vivid imagery.

Jeongjo had this *uigwe* (royal protocol) made after the procession to Hwaseong. Its title means "protocol for the procession to the royal tomb." *Uigwe* were produced to record the processes involved in state events and ceremonies. This one describes in detail the entire processes of the preparation and the procession itself, the names of those who took part, and financial information such as income and expenditure. Even the ingredients used to make each meal are recorded. Let's see what Lady Hyegyeong had for dinner on the first day: "rice with red beans, pollack soup, *jochi* (a kind of thick stew), sliced boiled meat, pickled fish, vegetables, kimchi, bean paste, fish dumplings, various fried dishes." The highlights of this *uigwe* are paintings of key scenes from the procession painted by artists in the Office of Court Painters under the supervision of Kim Hongdo. Their detailed, vivid depictions of moments like the crossing of the pontoon bridge, the full procession of 1,779 people, the celebration at Hwaseong and the military exercises are truly breathtaking.

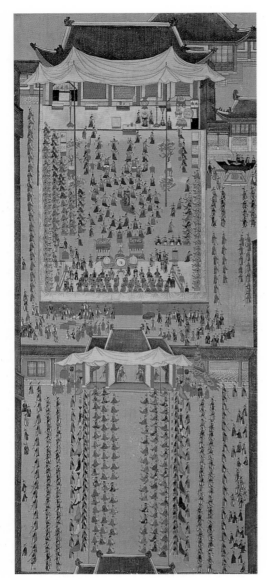

'Bongsudang jinchando'
('Illustration of the Celebration at Bongsudang Hall')
This painting shows a scene from the sixtieth birthday party of Lady Hyegyeong at Bongsudang Hall in Hwaseonghaenggung Temporary Palace. It's one of the illustrations included in *Wonhaeng eulmyo jeongni uigwe*.
–National Palace Museum of Korea

From then on, Mireukhyeon was known as Jijidaegogae Hill. A stele recording the origins of the name remains at the spot today.

Jeongjo stopped to talk with various commoners as he made his way back to Hanyang. He believed a king could never understand the troubles of his people if he spent all his time in a palace. He also thought that talking to his subjects would give them greater trust in their king, reinforcing his authority. On this note, the eight-day procession came to an end.

Why Jeongjo built Hwaseong

Hwaseong was an embodiment of Jeongjo's dreams: to eradicate factionalism in the royal court, reinforce his authority and improve the lives of his people. Among these, getting rid of factionalism was his top priority.

After taking the throne, Jeongjo set about gradually making his dream a reality. First of all, he established Gyujanggak, a royal library, and recruited young and talented officials regardless of their political faction—Noron, Soron, Namin, or whatever. He extended eligibility for government positions to the sons of concubines, based purely on merit. The king handpicked Park Jega, Yu Deukgong and Yi Deongmu as editor-compiler scholars at Gyujanggak, while devoting particular attention to talented officials such as Jeong Yagyong, earning their strong loyalty by giving them valuable books and entrusting them with important assignments.

Juhamnu Pavilion, Changdeokgung
The first floor of this pavilion housed Gyujanggak, Jeongjo's new royal library. On the inside, Gyujanggak was much more than a library: it was the nerve center of the king's new, reformed government. Books from the old library are now held at Kyujanggak Institute for Korean Studies at Seoul National University.

Next, the king created a new royal guard called the Jangyongyeong, which would be personally loyal to him. His units were stationed in both Hanyang and Hwaseong; that in the new city, in particular, was an elite force that enjoyed the special confidence of the king.

Gyujanggak and the Jangyongyeong constituted two wings, one civil and one military, that protected the king from both sides. Once these were in place, he began fulfilling his long-cherished ambition: the relocation of his father's tomb. At the time, Crown Prince Sado lay at the foot of Mt. Baebongsan in Yangju, Gyeonggi-do Province (the mountain behind what is now the University of Seoul); his son had the tomb transferred to Suwon and renamed it Hyeollyungwon.

Jeongjo's next move was to build a brand new city. Hwaseong would become the base from which the king

Jangyongyeong
This special military unit was set up by King Jeongjo for his own protection. It was divided between Hanyang and Hwaseong, with the former division named Jangyongnaeyeong (Inner Jangyongyeong) and the latter named Jangyongoeyeong (Outer Jangyongyeong).
But the new unit that the king had trusted so deeply was promptly abolished after his death.

developed a new kind of government. What exactly did this mean? Jeongjo wanted to be a "king like a moon illuminating myriad rivers." After eradicating the factionalism that had led to the death of his father, he would soar up into the sky and, like a moon shining light down on all the rivers and streams of the land, rule in an absolute yet fair and impartial manner that would ensure a good life for his people. Hwaseong would be the seat of this future government. This should give you some idea of why the new city meant so much to the king.

Construction of Hwaseong began in 1794, exactly 400 years after that of Hanyang. Though the original plan had envisaged a ten-year project, the city was completed in just two years and nine months.

Jeongjo planned to create prosperity in Hwaseong and boost its population by offering tax exemption to its citizens and various benefits to its merchants. At the time, Suwon was a small town with about 300 households and 1,500 inhabitants. Only one of the 300 homes had a tiled roof; all the rest were thatched. The building of the new city, however, produced an astonishing transformation.

Hwaseong made full use of the most advanced science, technology and culture of its time. The fortress wall that ran around it was rock-solid, fortified by a variety of observation towers and other new defensive features found nowhere else at the time. The wall provided the ideal defense against

● Hwaseong today

Seobuk Gongsimdon
With a name that means "hollow tower," this kind of feature is unique to Hwaseong. It is built from bricks and crowned with a wooden building for soldiers. Each floor has holes in its walls for firing guns.

Janganmun Gate
This is the palace's northern entrance, one of four main gates. It is the same size and shape as Paldalmun, its southern counterpart.

Hwahongmun Gate (northern water gate)
This beautiful viaduct over a clear stream was once used by local villagers as a place for washing clothes.

Hwaseomun Gate
Hwaseong's western gate.

Banghwa Suryujeong (northeastern watchtower)

Dongjangdae (command post and training ground)

Seojangdae Command Post
This command post stands in the west of Hwaseong; another stands in the east.

Palace

Naecheon Stream (Suwon Stream)

Changnyongmun Gate (eastern gate)

Hwayangnu Tower (southwestern watchtower)
Watchtowers like this were built on high points for surveying the surrounding area. This one, at the southwest of Hwaseong, as well as Banghwa Suryujeong in the northeast, also provide beautiful views.

Paldalmun Gate
The southern of Hwaseong's four main gates. The extra crescent wall outside the gate, known as a "ravelin," provides enhanced protection.

Bongdon Normally, just one of the five beacons atop this tower was kept lit. If an enemy appeared near one of Joseon's borders, a second would be fired up. Three lit beacons signaled that the enemy was approaching; four that it had crossed the border and invaded; and five that a war was in progress.

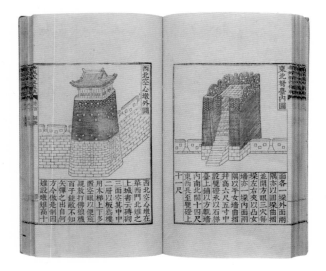

invading enemies.

Those working on the Hwaseong construction site were paid for their efforts. Though the government could have forced them to provide free labor, Jeongjo insisted that they be compensated and that he did not want a single worker to be exploited.

Jeongjo's death and the beginning of power politics

During the celebrations for his mother's sixtieth birthday at Hwaseong in the second February of 1795, Jeongjo had spoken:

"Ten years from now, when my mother turns seventy, we'll come back here for a rite at Hyeollyungwon and another party."

But the king's wish was never fulfilled: in 1800, just five

years after the Hwaseong procession, he suddenly died of a skin disease. Jeongjo's unexpected demise at the age of just forty-nine prompted rumors that the real cause of his death was not illness but deliberate poisoning. Members of the Namin faction, which was hit hard by the loss of the king, were particularly inclined to believe this version of events.

Jeongjo was succeeded by his eleven-year-old son, Crown Prince Sunjo. Now, Jeongsun, consort of the late king, took the reigns of power on behalf of the young monarch. The new regent destroyed everything that Jeongjo had achieved. She had the talented officials he had worked so hard to nurture executed or banished on charges such as believing in Western learning, and got rid of the Jangyongyeong altogether. Jeongjo's dream of uprooting factionalism and developing a new kind of politics now lay in tatters. Hwaseong, which still stands today, is the only remaining trace of his shattered vision.

After Jeongjo's death, political control fell into the hands of several influential clans such as the Kims of Andong, the Parks of Bannam and the Jos of Pungyang. Such domination of the royal court by a handful of powerful families is often known as "power politics"; in Joseon, it continued for the next sixty years, until the regency of Heungseon Daewongun.

King Jeongjo
This portrait is housed in Hwaryeongjeon Hall, where ancestral rites to King Jeongjo were held every year. The hall stands next to Hwaseonghaenggung.

New martial arts for Joseon

'Woldo' ('Moon sword')
This weapon was named for its crescent moon-shaped blade.

Around the time he relocated Crown Prince Sado's tomb to Suwon, Jeongjo summoned scholars Yi Deongmu and Park Jega of Gyujanggak and Baek Dongsu, an officer in the Jangyongyeong.

"I order you to compile a new martial arts manual," he said. "I've already decided the title: it'll be called *Muye dobo tongji* ('Comprehensive Illustrated Manual of Martial Arts')."

Jeongjo regarded martial arts as equally important to scholarship when it came to governing the country. If a king was to maintain his own power and keep a lid on factional strife, he needed the support of a reliable army. Believing it necessary to strike a balance between civil and military officialdoms, he often used to describe them as "the two wings of a bird, or the two wheels of a cart."

Jeongjo was not the first to attach such importance to martial arts: his father had shared this view. Though Sado's enemies in the Noron faction had portrayed him as weak and sensitive to the point of mental illness, he was in fact a strong and very brave man, skilled in his use of the heavy broadsword and highly accurate with a bow and arrow. Sado produced a book called *Muye sinbo* ("New Report on Martial Arts"). In some respects, then, Jeongjo's compilation of *Muye dobo tongji* was a continuation of his father's work.

As soon as Jeongjo died, however, Joseon martial arts went into sharp decline. Many of them disappeared entirely when Korea became a colony of Japan; only recently have some begun a revival in the guise of "traditional martial arts."

'Gwonbeop'
(A type of fist-based martial art)

●'Muye dobo tongji'

This book provides illustrated guides to the moves involved in twenty-four types of unique Joseon martial art based on a thorough review of the martial arts of Joseon, China and Japan. Each art is illustrated using diagrams accompanied by brief texts. The black and white pictures here are taken from *Muye dobo tongji*. The text was used as a training manual by all army units, including the Jangyongyeong and the Hullyeondogam (Military Training Agency). A copy was also published in Hangeul for soldiers who could not read classical Chinese.

'Ssanggeom' ('Two swords')

'Dangpa' ('Trident')
These men are fighting with three-pronged spears, known as tridents.

'Gichang' ('Lance')

'Deungpae' ('Wisteria shield')
As their name suggests, these shields are made from wisteria.

'Masang pyeongon' ('Horseback nunchuk')
This warrior wields a nunchuk as he rides his horse into battle. The nunchuk is similar in design to a flail used by farmers for threshing.

CHAPTER 2

The Silhak vision

Yu Hyeongwon placed the greatest emphasis on land reform in his book. Why?

"The huge estates of the rich stretch uninterrupted to the horizon and beyond, leaving nowhere for a commoner to stick so much as a pin in the ground," he wrote. "The rich merely grow richer, while the poor grow poorer. While crafty landowners monopolize the land, commoners drag their families around from place to place until their only option is to become farmhands."

TIME
LINE

1776

1780

1791

Joseon period
Jeongjo takes throne;
builds Gyujanggak

Park Jiwon travels to Qing;
writes *Yeolha ilgi*

'Keumnanjeongwon'
abolished except
for Yuguijeon

You may well have heard of Silhak, the reformist ideology that appeared in the late Joseon period. But why did it appear now? In the aftermath of the Japanese and Manchu invasions, Joseon found itself in need of change: a transformation that could solve the problems brought by war and inspire public spirit, which was in disarray.

How did the ruling class react to these circumstances? In fact, its members were stuck in their old, stale ways of thinking and failing to come up with solutions. In response, a number of figures began calling for various reforms that would improve the lives of the people: these were the so-called Silhak scholars.

Most of these reformists lived in the countryside, where they devoted themselves to study and research. None of them held high positions in the world of officialdom. This meant that their work did not become widely known and was not put into practice: all it could do was sit around in drawers and boxes, waiting to be discovered.

Still, the intentions and aspirations of the Silhak scholars were of some value in their own right.

Today, let's have a look at their beliefs and lives.

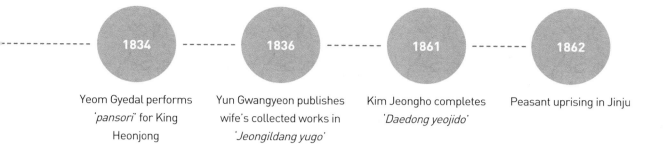

1834

Yeom Gyedal performs
'pansori' for King
Heonjong

1836

Yun Gwangyeon publishes
wife's collected works in
'Jeongildang yugo'

1861

Kim Jeongho completes
'Daedong yeojido'

1862

Peasant uprising in Jinju

Silhak scholars first emerged around the seventeenth century. These figures believed academic study should be of use in real life: the word Silhak literally means "practical learning." In this respect, they differed considerably from Neo-Confucian scholars of their time, who were bogged down in arguments about moral duty and failed to come up anything that was of much help to those living in the real world.

Even among Silhak scholars, interests varied from one individual to another. Some focused on agriculture, an integral part of the lives of commoners, and called for land reform; among them were figures such as Yu Hyeongwon, Yi Ik and Jeong Yagyong.

Others asserted the need to develop commerce in Joseon,

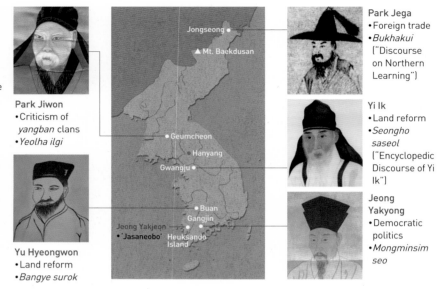

Silhak scholars: their key arguments and works
These thinkers studied practical subjects relevant to everyday life, calling for various reforms aimed at solving real problems. Here are some of their major texts and achievements.

Park Jiwon
- Criticism of *yangban* clans
- *Yeolha ilgi*

Yu Hyeongwon
- Land reform
- *Bangye surok*

Park Jega
- Foreign trade
- *Bukhakui* ("Discourse on Northern Learning")

Yi Ik
- Land reform
- *Seongho saseol* ("Encyclopedic Discourse of Yi Ik")

Jeong Yakyong
- Democratic politics
- *Mongminsim seo*

Map labels: Jongseong, Mt. Baekdusan, Geumcheon, Hanyang, Gwangju, Buan, Gangjin, Jeong Yakjeon, 'Jasaneobo', Heuksando Island

claiming that their countrymen should not look down on Qing as a barbarian empire but learn certain things from it. Scholars who advocated learning from the ways of Qing were known collectively as the Bukhak ("Northern learning") faction and included Park Jiwon, Park Jega and Hong Daeyong.

Still other scholars studied the history, geography and languages of the Korean Peninsula: among their number were historian An Jeongbok; Kim Jeongho, creator of the famous map *Daedong yeojido*; and Yu Hui and Sin Gyeongjun, who studied Hangeul.

Here, I'd like to tell you about Yu Hyeongwon, Jeong Yagyong and Park Jiwon, three of the leading Silhak scholars.

Silhak pioneer: Yu Hyeongwon

Yu Hyeongwon influenced a number of other Silhak scholars.
This is why he's sometimes known as the pioneer of Silhak.
His father died after getting caught up in factional strife when
Yu was just two years old; from then on, the boy was brought
up by his grandfather.

Born and raised in Hanyang, Yu moved to Uban-dong in
Buan, Jeolla-do Province at the age of thirty-two. He had
turned his back on the state examination and a potential
career in government and chosen to live in the countryside
instead. Uban-dong had once been the home of his
grandfather, too.

How did Yu spend his new rural life? In his house, which

stood in the middle of a bamboo grove, he passed every day reading the books handed down by his ancestors until late at night. They say he had some 10,000 books there.

But Yu had not moved to the countryside simply to study. His intention was to live among the peasants, observing their lives for himself, and come up with solutions to the problems of Joseon society. Yu possessed a sense of duty that told him this was what men of learning ought to do.

Finally, after twenty years combining study with observation of the lives of peasants, Yu put forth his own thoughts in the form of a book titled *Bangye surok*. Bangye was Yu's pen name, taken from the name of a stream that flowed near Uban-dong, while *surok* describes a running record of thoughts, written down as they occur. Yu placed the greatest emphasis on land reform in his book. Why?

"The huge estates of the rich stretch uninterrupted to the horizon and beyond, leaving nowhere for a commoner to stick so much as a pin in the ground," he wrote. "The rich merely grow richer, while the poor grow poorer. While crafty landowners monopolize the land, commoners drag their families around from place to place until their only option is to become farmhands."

The Joseon land system worked fundamentally to the advantage of *yangban* aristocrats rather than peasants. After the Japanese and Manchu invasions, instances of *yangban*

Peasants and land
Joseon was an agricultural society in which farming was the principal source of most people's livelihood. Agriculture and land reform were intimately connected. Living standards for peasants were determined by whether the land system worked to their advantage or to that of the *yangban*. In the latter case, the peasants always ended up grindingly poor and hungry, no matter how hard they worked.

Yu Hyeongwon calls for land reform
"As long as the land system is not put right, the lives of the people will remain unstable, chaos will reign in all state systems, and politics and education will fall into neglect. The land is the principle foundation of the state; if this foundation collapses, everything will be plunged into disorder." Despite this claim, Yu's reform plan was never put into action.

monopolizing land became more frequent. When this happened, poor peasants were left with no land to farm, and had to borrow that of *yangban*, who took most of their tenants' harvest as rent. This meant that peasants, no matter how hard they worked, stood no chance of accumulating wealth of any kind; in fact, they grew poorer as time passed.

The poorer its peasants, the poorer the state became. This was because peasants were also the most important taxpayers, while *yangban* enjoyed tax exemption at the time.

Yu Hyeongwon believed the status quo, if left unchanged, would lead to the downfall of both the peasants and the state. This is why he called for land reform.

So what were the details of Yu's reform plan? He advocated nationalizing all the land in Joseon, then distributing it equally among the country's peasants. This, he believed, would eliminate social inequality.

Bangye surok also contains plans for reform in a variety of other fields, including the state examination and the slavery system. It is, in other words, Yu's blueprint for a newly designed Joseon. Yu, however, died three years after completing his book.

After Yu's death, his students sent *Bangye surok* to officials in Hanyang, but the capital's bureaucrats didn't even bother looking at it. It was only seventy years later, during the reign of King Yeongjo, that Yu's text saw the light of day again. Yeongjo himself read the book, recognized its value and had it circulated among his ministers in the royal court and officials in the provinces.

Social criticism in the form of a novel: Park Jiwon

Park Jiwon was born into a family that belonged to the Noron faction, which had emerged victorious in the most recent power struggle at the royal court.

Park was far from an ordinary Noron *yangban*, however. Uninterested in taking the state examination or gaining a government position, he put off taking the test until the relatively advanced age of thirty-four, whereupon he barely managed to enter, then ended up passing as the highest-scoring candidate. Even then, he gave up any ambition of a

The novels of Park Jiwon
Park wrote several novels in which the protagonists were looked down upon for their low social status, but were in fact morally superior to *yangban* in terms of both thoughts and actions. These include works such as *Yedeok Seonsaeng jeon* ("The Tale of Mr. Yedeok"), which praises the diligence of a night soil disposal man; *Gwangmunja jeon* ("Gwangmun: The Autobiography"), which praises the honesty of a beggar named Gwangmun; and *Yeollyeo Hamyang Bakssi jeon* ("The Tale of Lady Park of Hamyang, Woman of Virtue"), which depicts the hard life of a widow who is forced to remain chaste after her husband dies.

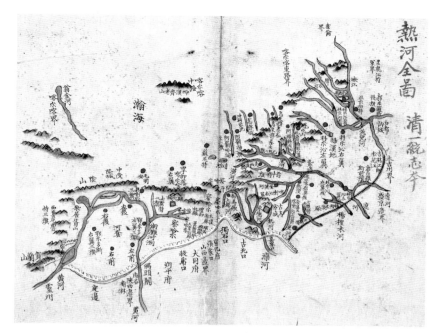

'Yeolha jeondo' ('Complete map of Jehol')
Park Jiwon's delegation traveled a long way to attend the Qing Emperor's birthday celebrations. He wrote down everything that had happened from the moment it crossed the Amnokgang River, passing through Liaodong, reaching Beijing, then traveling to Jehol and back to Beijing again—a journey of about two months—in a book called *Yeolha ilgi*. Yeolha is the Korean pronunciation of Jehol, the region to the northeast of Beijing where the emperor's summer palace was located. It corresponds to the area around what is now Chengde in China's Hebei Province.
−The National Library of Korea

career in government.

In his actions, too, Park was utterly unlike most other *yangban*, who tended to be rather self-important. He would go without eating for several days at a time, rarely washed and would freely associate with farmhands, merchants and woodcutters—the kind of people disdained by other *yangban* for being low class. He even took his entire family out of Hanyang and went to live in Yeonam Valley in Geumcheon, Hwanghae-do Province, where they spent nine years as farmers. This is where his pen name, Yeonam, came from.

While Park was living in Yeonam Valley, his third cousin, Park Myeongwon, was sent as a government envoy to Qing. Park Jiwon was given a place in his cousin's entourage and accompanied him on the journey. He wrote an account of his experience in Qing, which he titled *Yeolha ilgi* ("Jehol Journal") and used to make the argument that Joseon should not simply look down upon Qing as a barbarian state but attempt to learn certain things from it.

Most Joseon *yangban* at the time regarded Qing as a barbarian country and advocated a so-called "subjugation of the North": a Joseon expedition to conquer Qing. It came to others as a big shock, then, when Park called instead for "Bukhak" and claimed that Joseon actually had something to learn from its giant neighbor.

Park also claimed that commerce should be encouraged, rather than looked down upon, despite the fact that most *yangban* at the time did not regard it as a respectable occupation.

Park attracted a following of some of Joseon's best and brightest young scholars thanks to his reputation as an outstanding writer. His stories criticize *yangban* for the way they devote themselves to preening and keeping up appearances while making life a misery for commoners. Such works include *Yangban jeon* ("Tale of a Yangban"), *Hojil* ("The Roar of a Tiger") and *Heosaeng jeon* ("The Tale of Mr. Heo"). Let's take a look at a passage from *Yangban jeon*:

"When heaven created the people, it made four different kinds. The most noble among these were the classical scholars, whom we call *yangban*. Nothing is better than being a *yangban*. You don't have to farm or sell anything. ... Even if you live in the countryside, you can do what you want. You can take your neighbor's cow and plow your own fields first, or summon the other villagers to weed them first. Even then, no one is allowed to say anything. And no one can hold it against you even if you pour lye up his nose, twist his top-knot and pluck his beard off."

Park was stinging in his criticism of the tyranny of *yangban*. His stories are great fun to read, even today. At the time, however, he was shunned by other *yangban* for his undignified behavior. While Park's works were originally

 Hong Daeyong, the man who claimed that the earth rotates

The people of Joseon believed earth was square and the sky was round. Hardly anyone thought earth itself could be round. But Silhak scholar Hong Daeyong was an exception. He also believed that his home planet spun around by itself. In a book titled *Uisan mundap* ("Dialogue on Mt. Yiwulüshan"), he argued as follows:

"The earth is round in shape and drifts continuously in the void. ... It turns around once each day; its circumference is 90,000 *ri* and one day lasts 12 hours. To turn through 90,000 *ri* in 12 hours, it must spin at a speed faster than lighting or a cannonball."

But what Hong didn't know was that the earth orbited the sun. He believed the earth was at the center of the cosmos, that it spun by itself, and that the sun and moon orbited it. This notion was similar to the theory of a Western astronomer by the name of Tycho Brahe. Perhaps Hong was indeed aware of Brahe's theory, which had reached Qing by that time.

written in classical Chinese, they have now been translated into Korean, making them much more accessible.

Drawing the strands of Silhak together:
Jeong Yagyong

While Park Jiwon used fictional works to deliver his criticisms of society, Jeong Yagyong studied ways to reform it. And while Park was born into a family that belonged to the victorious Noron faction, Jeong came from a defeated Namin background.

At the age of sixteen, Jeong was deeply inspired by a book written by Silhak scholar Yi Ik. Though Yi himself was already dead by then, Jeong was able to learn about his thought from his great-grandson, Yi Gahwan, who was a relative of Jeong.

Jeong passed the state examination at the age of twenty-eight and began a career in government, where he became a highly valued and trusted protégé of King Jeongjo. Over the next decade he worked his way through several government positions while remaining a favorite of the reform-minded monarch.

Jeong, however, was considerably different to other scholars. As well as studying Neo-Confucianism in depth, he read about and gained a thorough knowledge of subjects to which most of his fellow academics paid no attention whatsoever, such as architecture, mathematics, medicine, geography and science. This was probably due to the influence of Yi Ik, who took an interest in the practical demands of everyday life.

Model of a crane
The design for this crane was inspired by a book called *Qiqi tushou* ("Illustrations and Explanations of Wonderful Machines"), a copy of which was given to Jeong Yagyong by King Jeongjo. *Qiqi tushou* was written by Terrentius Constantiensis, a German Jesuit missionary, and Wang Zheng, a Ming scholar. Its full title is *Yuanxi qiqi tushuo luzui* ("Diagrams and Explanations of the Wonderful Machines of the Far West").

Jeong Yagyong played key roles in the building of Hwaseong, Jeongjo's ambitious new city, and in the royal procession to it. He drew sketches for the entire development and made detailed plans for how the fortress would be built, what facilities it would include, and so on. As part of this process, he created cranes for lifting heavy stones, easing the strain on the workers building the fortress. He was involved in the building of the pontoon bridge over the Hangang. And he took part in every part of the procession to Hwaseong, as an official in the Ministry of Defense.

Members of the dominant Noron faction were jealous of the way Jeong enjoyed such high favor from the king. They wasted no time in badmouthing him whenever the opportunity arose. Around this time, Jeong was immersing himself in Seohak, the study of Catholicism and other Western culture. Seohak had reached Joseon by way of Qing, and was banned by the government at the time. The state

Jeong Yagyong's studies
Jeong's studies fall into two main categories: social reform and a search for the original spirit of Confucianism. Scholars at the time adhered to Neo-Confucianism, the philosophy synthesized by Zhu Xi of Song China. But Jeong believed it was necessary to go back to an earlier version of Confucianism; namely, that originally created by Confucius himself. The call for a return to the teachings of Confucius was at the very core of Silhak thought.

Jeong Yagyong's birthplace
Jeong was born in this house in Majae (now Neungnae-ri in Namyangju-gun County, Gyeonggi-do Province). The sign above the door reads "Yeoyudang" in Sino-Korean characters. While *dang* means "hall," *yeoyu* refers to a stanza from the *Daodejing* that reads, "Hesitate as if crossing a frozen river in winter; waver as if danger lurks in all directions."

had decreed that only Neo-Confucianism was correct, and forbade belief in anything else on the grounds that it was heresy.

Despite this, Seohak was secretly spreading through Joseon society; nowhere was this happening faster than among members of the Namin faction, which had lost power in the struggle against its Noron nemesis. Several people regarded Seohak not as a religious faith but as a system of thought closely related to new Western culture, and were studying it with interest. Curious about the new influx of knowledge, they read their way through various Seohak texts.

Whenever a rumor went around that Jeong believed in Seohak, Jeongjo took his side and protected him. As soon as the king died, however, Jeong was sent into exile in Gangjin, Jeolla-do Province for the crime of dabbling in the new Western knowledge.

Jeong was just one of a string of scholars to be punished for their association with Seohak. In fact, however, Catholicism was just a pretext used by the Noron faction to get rid of the Namin. As I've just mentioned, many members of the latter faction were Catholics.

Jeong was lucky enough to get away only with exile, but Yakjong, his older brother, and Yi Seunghun, his brother-in-law, were put to death, while Yi Gahwan died in prison and Yakjeon, another of Jeong's elder brothers, died in exile on far-flung Heuksan-do Island.

Jeong's life of banishment began when he was forty and lasted a full eighteen years. The scholar spent this long stretch of time observing the lives of the commoners around him and considering ways of enabling both the state and its people to prosper.

In Jeong's view, the three most fundamental problems faced by Joseon were its land system, its tax regime and official corruption. What, then, must be done to create a healthy, prosperous state and high living standards for its people? Jeong immersed himself in study, reading book after book in search of an answer to this question.

Finally, he wrote down the results of his study in several books. Being in exile, he had no chance to take action

Dasan Chodang
This is the house where Jeong Yagyong spent his years in exile. It is located in the village of Gyul-dong in Gangjin, Jeollanam-do. It was here that Jeong wrote many books during his eighteen years in exile. Dasan was Jeong's pen name, while *chodang* means "thatched house." Though originally thatched, the house was rebuilt in 1958 with a tiled roof.

Jeong Yakjeon
The second-eldest of the Jeong brothers, Yakjeon was banished to a remote island off the south coast for the crime of believing in Seohak. Moving between islands such as Sinjido, Uido and Heuksando, he wrote *Jasan eobo* ("Encyclopedia of Heuksando Fish") based upon his observations of several hundred fish and other sea creatures found in the local area. The book is also sometimes known as *Hyeonsan eobo* (both Jasan and Hyeonsan are alternative names for Heuksan). Jeong Yakjeon died on Uido in 1816.

'Yeoyudang jip' ('Yeoyudang Compilation')
This book is a compilation of the complete works of Jeong Yagyong. It contains the 'One Design and Two Books,' as well as all of Jeong's other works on subjects such as science, medicine and even poetry. Yeoyudang was the name of the house in which Jeong was born; he sometimes also used it as one of his pen names.
– Kyujanggak Institute for Korean Studies

himself; all he could do was write down his ideas and hope somebody would put them to use one day. Three of the most important of books are titled *Gyeongse yupyo* ("Design for Good Government"), *Mongminsim seo* ("Admonitions on Governing the People") and *Heumheum sinseo* ("Toward a New Jurisprudence"); together, they are known as the "One Design and Two Books". *Gyeongse yupyo* contains Jeong's proposed method for rectifying systems of national government; *Mongminsim seo* outlines the ideal way for the governor of a county to govern its people; and *Heumheum sinseo* describes how to administer fair punishment. In *Mongminsim seo*, Jeong wrote, "The governor is there for the people, not the other way round."

Jeong produced more than 500 other books in addition to these. Collectively, his works cover all the core areas of Silhak, which is why he is often regarded as the man who achieved synthesis in the movement.

By the time Jeong was freed from exile and returned to his hometown he was an old man, not far from his sixtieth birthday. He now wrote the following note, asking that it be put into his coffin with him when he died:

"I've written on the Six Classics and the Four Books, which can be used for personal cultivation, and authored the One Design and Two Books for governing the world and the country. Everything necessary is in there, from beginning to end. But since many people condemn my books and few understand them, please just burn them all if Heaven prevents them being put to use."

This quote illustrates Jeong's regret at the way his research, the product of so much hard work, had not yet been put to use. He passed away at the age of seventy-five, without a chance to enter government again.

'Wealth is created by the people'

"Wealth does not fall from the sky: it is the product of the blood and sweat of the people. If the people prosper, so does the state. ... The state appoints officials for the sake of the people. If you ask an official about his job, he'll answer that it is to be like a father to them. But his behavior is more like that of their enemy. Commoners are unable to use the crops they grow and the items they produce, using all their wisdom and strength, to support their parents, wives and children. Instead, they have to get down on their knees and surrender it to these enemies. They might as well let the sparrows eat all the ripened grain in the fields and invite the rats into their storehouses to finish off the rest."

These are the words of Silhak scholar Yi Ik, written in his book *Seongho saseol*. Yi, like Yu Hyeongwon, was an advocate of land reform. He believed the lives of the people could only be stabilized through land reform to restore balance to the agricultural system.

But Yi's proposed land reform differed somewhat to that of Yu: he proposed determining the minimum area of land needed by each household, calling such basic plots *yeongeopjeon* ("working land held in perpetuity"). Once these areas had been established, households in possession of more than their calculated areas would be forbidden from buying new land, while those with less than the minimum area would be encouraged to buy more. Yi claimed

'Seongho saseol'
Yi Ik never took a government position, spending his life surrounded by books instead. His works include *Seongho saseol* and *Gwagu rok* ("Record of Concern for the Underprivileged").
– Kyujanggak Institute for Korean Studies

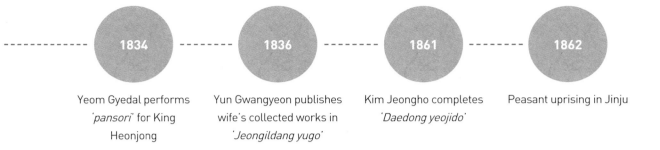

Rice transplantation came to Joseon as a new farming technique that involves sowing rice seeds in specially-made seed trays, waiting for them to sprout, then transplanting the seedlings to a paddy. Before transplantation was introduced, seeds were simply sown straight into the paddy from day one.

Transplantation: a revolutionary new technique

Today is transplanting day in Yi Sundol's paddy. Sundol gets up early and hurries down to the field, where he finds his neighbors already waiting. Transplantation requires an intensive burst of work in a short period of time; more than can be done by just one or two pairs of hands. In Joseon, this

'Dure'

Dure is the traditional custom of sharing labor among villagers when it comes to hard jobs like rice transplanting and weeding. It's also the name of organizations formed for such group work. Dure groups were made up of strong, healthy village men. When their work together was done, they sometimes played music and had a party.

is made possible by a system where neighbors gather and work together on one paddy each day: yours today, mine tomorrow and so on. This sharing of work among neighbors is called *dure* or *pumasi* in Korean.

Remember how I told you rice seeds were planted directly in fields before transplantation was introduced? The new system brought huge advantages.

Firstly, it required fewer rounds of weeding, and less effort in each weeding session. (Weeding, as you know, was done in order to leave all the soil's nutrients for the rice itself.)

When rice was transplanted, far fewer weeds grew than when it was simply sown directly into the paddy. The old system had required four of five rounds of weeding every summer; transplantation cut this number to just two or three. Weeding a paddy all day under the relentless midsummer sun is quite an ordeal. Anyone who's sweated through such an experience knows just how good it feels to avoid even one or two rounds of it a year.

Secondly, transplantation allows double-cropping: two crops in every paddy, every year. After the rice is harvested in autumn, barley is harvested in the empty field. The barley is then harvested the following year, before the next lot of rice seedlings is transplanted.

When rice was still grown by direct seeding, rice seeds had to be sown earlier than what would have been the barley harvesting season: the timing, in other words, didn't allow double-cropping. Rice is sown in March and harvested in August, according to the lunar calendar, while barley is sown in September and harvested in April the next year: the two crops' seasons overlap by a month in spring. But the transplantation system leaves paddies empty from the rice harvest until May the next year, giving more than enough time for a crop of barley.

The barley grown under the double cropping system filled a crucial gap, providing much needed food in the traditionally lean spring season. You may have heard of the "barley hump," a name used to describe the time of year when all of last year's rice has run out and this year's barley has not yet ripened. This annual period of hunger was so-called because all the farmers could do to endure it was pin their hopes on the barley as they watched it slowly ripen

'Sesipungsokdo'
('seasoual genre painting')
This painting shows scenes of spring in a Joseon farming village, with cows pulling plows and villagers hard at work.
– Dong-A University Museum

in the fields. "If I can only make it over this hump, I'll fill my stomach with a bowl of fresh barley," they told themselves.

After hours of transplanting seedlings, Yi Sundol finally straightens his back and looks up at the sky. It's a beautiful shade of blue.

"Better be a good harvest again this year," he mutters.

Despite its many advantages, rice transplantation also had a huge drawback: it required water. Without this essential commodity, transplanted rice seedlings wouldn't grow properly. If a drought occurred in May, the transplanting season, an entire year's crop would be ruined. And in Korea, May droughts are far from rare.

In fact, rice transplantation had been used as a technique in some regions earlier in the Joseon period. But the state ended up banning it because of the danger of drought ruining the whole harvest.

Farmers, however, came up with a way of beating droughts. They built reservoirs, then used the water stored there to irrigate their paddies if it failed to rain in time for the

Preparing to transplant rice
Villagers worked collectively when transplanting rice, laboring together in each household's paddy in turn. This man is using a dipper to flood the field that must be next in line for rice transplanting. The man in the foreground is carrying a pot of urine for use as fertilizer, while the woman in the distance has a basket of food on her head. Villagers had to work non-stop.

transplanting season. Most farmers now abandoned the old method of sowing seeds directly, knowing that transplantation brought much more rice as long as they had a reliable supply of water.

There was another disadvantage to rice transplantation: double-cropping exhausted the nutrients in the soil much faster, rendering it unable to produce good harvests. Farmers got around this problem, too, by using manure to restore lost fertility.

All this should give you some idea of the resourcefulness of Joseon's farmers. Rice transplantation wouldn't have got far without reservoirs and fertilizer. Thanks to the development of these techniques, however, it took off across the country.

"Right, that's enough for today."

Yi snaps out of his reverie at the words of Chilbok's grandfather. The sun is already starting to sink. Tomorrow, they'll finish transplanting the rice into his field. The day after that, it will be the turn of Chilbok's family.

Dipper
This tool was used to scoop water from low areas to higher ground. The handle was raised when filling the hollow area with water, then pushed down to raise and pour it into a field or channel above.
– National Folk Museum of Korea

Urine pot
Pots like this were used for carrying urine to paddies for use as fertilizer. Human and animal excrement was excellent for this purpose. Nobody would waste valuable manure by using the toilet when visiting the neighbors.

Dry-field farming brings new hope

Rice transplanting made the life of farmers far less exhausting than it had been. It saved them plenty of time, too. In fact, the transplantation method demanded about forty percent less time and energy than direct seeding had done. What had once required ten hours' work a day now took only six.

So what did farmers do with their newly liberated four hours each day? Far from letting it go to waste, they used it to grow as much extra grain as they could. They double-cropped, put more energy into dry-field farming, and, when they were able to save up a little, bought more land for cultivation.

While rice transplantation was breathing new life into paddy farming, dry-field agriculture was enjoying a renaissance of its own. Here, too, a new method brought change: farmers began using a deeper plowing technique to create ridges and furrows; they then sowed seeds in the latter. Like rice transplantation in paddy fields, the new ridge and furrow method roughly halved the amount of effort required by dry-field farming. It stopped seeds from dying even in the coldest depths of winter and the harshest summer droughts, and made weeding much easier.

Dry-field agriculture brought new hope to the peasants of Joseon. They were able to spend much more time on it thanks to the savings brought by rice transplantation. Growing crops like cotton, tobacco and vegetables in dry fields and selling them at markets allowed farmers to earn more money than by growing only rice.

Rice grown in paddies was not meant to be sold. It was used to feed families for the year and to pay rent to landlords and tax to the state. And some had to be kept aside as seed for next year's crop. Most produce grown in dry fields, on the other hand, was destined for sale at markets.

Villages located near big cities could make a lot of money by growing and selling vegetables, since city dwellers had to buy their food. Water parsley, Chinese cabbages, cucumbers and chilies were all popular commodities. Before long, some vegetables from certain villages developed reputations for being particularly fresh and tasty. Examples include Chinese cabbages and water parsley from Wangsimni, and daikon radish from Salgoji (the area around today's Seongsu-dong and Jayang-dong neighborhoods in Seoul).

Tobacco was also a popular commodity, having entered Joseon after the Japanese invasions. Though it seems absurd today, a rumor at the time that the leaf was

Plowing a field
This detail from a painting by artist Kim Hongdo shows a pair of oxen pulling a plow. The plow is an age-old farming tool; when it is used to create deep furrows, the grain or vegetable seeds planted in them grow better. Horses were used to pull plows, too.
- National Museum of Korea

Cutting tobacco
This picture shows one man trimming big tobacco leaves and another slicing them with a guillotine. The figure below on the left sits in front of a book, fanning himself. Is he reading it to the others to keep them entertained as they work? This work is also by Kim Hongdo.
–National Museum of Korea

good at killing roundworms in the stomach encouraged pretty much everyone—young, old, female and male—to smoke. Naturally, such high demand drove up tobacco prices. Growing a successful crop brought enough income to keep a family fed all year round.

Several regions also developed their own specialties, such as Hansan ramie, Jeonju ginger and Gangjin sweet potatoes.

Five-day markets

Now that farmers were growing plenty of cash crops, a new market culture emerged with the increased trade in such commodities. By the late Joseon period, markets had appeared all over the country; in the mid-eighteenth century, there were more than 1,000 nationwide.

Markets at the time were very different to those we know now, which are open every day. You and I can buy what we need by popping down to the market at any time except Sundays, but Joseon markets only opened on certain days. Most took place every five days and were therefore known, logically enough, as five-day markets.

Have you ever heard the Korean phrase, "meeting the market by chance?" We use it when somebody unexpectedly comes across something good. Of course, such a phrase would never have come into existence if markets had been held every day.

So what did people do when they needed to buy something urgently? They had to go to another village where a market was being held that day. Since nearby villages held markets on different days to avoid overlap, you could generally buy what you needed if you were prepared to invest the necessary legwork.

Markets were meeting places as well as hubs of trade. In the days long before telephones and the Internet, friends who lived far apart would come together on market day.

Another commodity traded at markets was information. All kinds of news were exchanged between friends and relatives as they chatted busily over bowls of noodles and rice soup. Many restaurants in Korea still serve "market noodles" or "market rice soup," indicating the pleasure and fond memories associated with the marketplace to this day.

Marketplaces also provided a venue for lively festivals with plenty to see and eat.

The history of markets
Markets have existed since the distant past. *Samguk sagi* records how a market called the Gyeongsasi was held in Gyeongju as far back as the fifth century, in the Silla period. In the Goryeo period, too, the capital, Gaegyeong, hosted markets full of big and small stalls. They began as places for bartering goods; later on, money gradually emerged as an intermediary means of selling and buying.

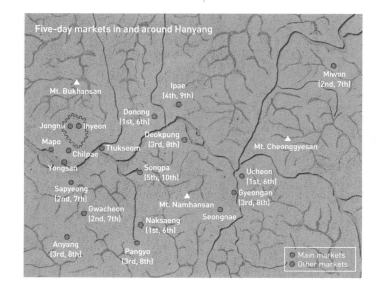

Five-day markets in and around Hanyang

Miwon (2nd, 7th)
Mt. Bukhansan
Ipae (4th, 9th)
Donong (1st, 6th)
Jongnu Ihyeon
Mapo
Chilpae Ttukseom
Deokpung (3rd, 8th)
Mt. Cheonggyesan
Yongsan
Songpa (5th, 10th)
Ucheon (1st, 6th)
Sapyeong (2nd, 7th)
Gyeongan (3rd, 8th)
Mt. Namhansan
Gwacheon (2nd, 7th)
Naksaeng (1st, 6th)
Seongnae
Anyang (3rd, 8th)
Pangyo (3rd, 8th)
Main markets
Other markets

'Market'

Markets, past and present, are lively, bustling places. Joseon markets were like festivals—even those who had nothing in particular to buy must have enjoyed going just to look around or share a hot bowl of rice soup with an old friend. This is *Sijang* ("Market"), a genre painting by artist Kim Jungeun.

Itinerant vendors

These traveling traders are known by a variety of names in Korean, many of which refer to the different ways they would carry their wares from one market to the next: some stacked goods on rigid A-frames that they bore on their backs, while others wrapped them in large cloths known as *bojagi* to create large bundles that they lugged around in their arms or in shoulder bags.

Sometimes, a display of masked dancing or tightrope walking would be put on to attract more shoppers.

Yet another function of markets was for gatherings and rallies—they were unbeatable as meeting places. Many of the peasant uprisings in late Joseon began with marketplace gatherings.

Itinerant vendors

Market vendors included both peasants selling their own produce and professional traders. The latter would travel around from market to market: here one day, there the next. They were known as itinerant vendors.

The many items sold by itinerant vendors ranged from fabrics like cotton and ramie, fish, salt, cast iron pots, wooden bowls, bamboo baskets and other everyday items to various more expensive goods.

Though some itinerant vendors were wealthy, most were too poor even to have a place to live. Such poor vendors would take their wives and children with them from one village to another, selling their goods as they traveled. It was a very tough way of life.

Itinerant vendors set off for the next village
The market in the village below is over, and now these traders are crossing a mountain to get to the next village. The journey is a hard one, but the hope of selling more wares at tomorrow's market keeps them going.

Thanks to itinerant vendors, new paths kept appearing. These included the road between Joryeong and Jungnyeong, the road over the mountain pass between Cheongju and Sangju, the

'Jumak' ('Inn') by Kim Hongdo
–National Museum of Korea

 'Sijeon' and 'nanjeon'

Hanyang was home to a special kind of shop called a *sijeon*. Anyone wanting to sell goods in the capital was not allowed to trade directly with customers: instead, he or she had to first hand the goods to a *sijeon*. Anyone ignoring the *sijeon* and dealing directly with consumers was accused of engaging in *nanjeon* and would have her or his goods seized by *sijeon* merchants and be punished or fined. Let's say your mother was critically ill and you had to urgently make some money to buy her medicine. You went out with a piece of good silk you had been saving and tried to sell it. Immediately, a *sijeon* merchant would pop up and begin shouting at you for *nanjeon* and knocking over all your stuff. He'd even take your silk away. This kind of thing happened on a daily basis.

This special right of *sijeon* merchants was known as *geumnanjeongwon*, meaning "the right to forbid *nanjeon*." It was accorded by the state. Why? In exchange for providing the goods needed in royal palaces and government offices, or as gifts for foreign states.

The largest *sijeon*, of which there were between six and eight, were known collectively as the Yuguijeon. These included the Seonjeon and the Myeonjujeon, both of which sold silk; the Jeopojeon, which sold ramie; the Myeonpojeon, which sold cotton fabric; the Cheongpojeon, which sold woolen goods; the Eomuljon, which sold fish products; and the Jijeon, which sold paper. Most of the Yuguijeon were gathered along Unjongga, the central Seoul street now known as Jongno.

Ihwaryeong Pass road linking Goesan and Mungyeong, and many more.

Taverns invariably sprang up along roads like these, offering traveling vendors the chance to have a meal, replace their worn-out straw shoes and rest their weary legs.

When the sun went down, they would all lie down in the large, shabby guest room and go to sleep. The next day, they would set off again at sunrise. Sometimes, on hard, lonely journeys, they sang songs like this one to comfort themselves:

Feet bound, hat on my head.

Spare sandals on my belt, a load on my back.

I hurry from one market to the next

meeting my fellow peddlers.

Passing on the latest news, picking up more,

we laugh and shout.

Come rain or shine, we walk on, chatting all the way.

When the sun goes down

we join hands and say our goodbyes.

See you at the next market tomorrow!

Peddler
This traveling vendor, his A-frame stacked high with earthenware, has stopped for a quick rest.

'Sanga yorok': A royal physician's cookbook

Royal doctors were the highest ranking and best paid figures in the entire medical profession. *Sanga yorok* ("Compendium of Information on Living in the Mountains") is a recipe book written by Jeon Sunui, King Sejo's physician. You may find it strange that a doctor wrote such a book, but he did so in the belief that food itself was the best medicine. In Joseon, doctors who used food to cure their patients were held in higher esteem than those who used medicine. So Jeon's book was actually more of a medical text than a cookbook of the sort we know.

Curing illness by way of diet was known in Korean as *sikchi*, literally meaning "food healing." King Sejong suffered from an ailment known as *sogaljeung*, which is thought to have been what we now call diabetes. His doctor advised him to eat chicken and pheasant, both of which were said to be effective against *sogaljeung*, telling the king that food, rather than medicine, should be used to cure him. Other foods eaten by the king for medical purposes included *yakbap* (rice cooked with a mixture of honey, dates, chestnuts and other ingredients), *kongjang* (seasoned soy beans), and *jeonyak* (herbal decoctions).

In addition to functioning as medical texts, Joseon cookbooks such as *Sanga yorok* were also food encyclopedias, full of information on all things edible, and farming encyclopedias, providing details of how to sow and cultivate a variety of crops.

Sanga yorok contains a method for growing vegetables in the middle of winter. The technique is roughly akin to a modern greenhouse, but consists of a mud hut with a south-facing opening to provide maximum sunlight and

an underfloor *ondol* heating system to provide warmth. Just imagine that: a greenhouse, 550 years ago. This was 170 years before the German greenhouse that is generally considered to have been the world's first.

CHAPTER 4

Popular culture flourishes

Pansori began among *cheonmin*. *Pansori* entertainers traveled around, performing at busy places like markets and farming villages. As word got around that their shows were great fun to watch, however, they found themselves invited increasingly often to perform in wealthy homes. Soon, some *yangban* started performing *pansori* themselves.

1776

Joseon period
Jeongjo takes throne;
builds Gyujanggak

1780

Park Jiwon travels to Qing;
writes *Yeolha ilgi*

1791

'Keumnanjeongwon'
abolished except
for Yuguijeon

You may recall how I described the late Joseon period as a time of change. Among the most striking of the many transformations in progress at this time was the emergence of ordinary people as the stars of art and culture.

Culture and art created and driven by commoners is described as "popular" in order to distinguish it from the yangban-dominated culture that came before it.

Before the emergence of popular culture, commoners had had neither the time nor resources to devote to culture or the arts. Now, though, new developments in farming and commerce brought better living standards, and ordinary people began turning their attention to what had previously been beyond their reach.

So what kinds of culture were popular at this time? Pansori, Hangeul novels, masked dances and folk paintings are all prime examples.

Popular culture was distinct from yangban culture in several ways: it contained honest expressions of the thoughts and feelings of the people, and it criticized the problems of society while remaining highly upbeat rather than gloomy or tinged with despair. It was full of humor, in other words.

Today, let's have a look at popular culture in late Joseon.

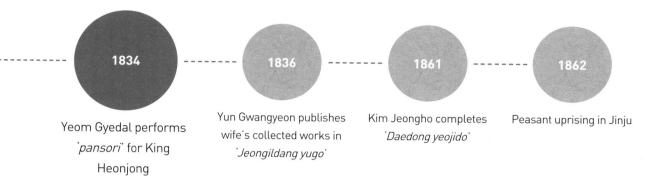

1834

Yeom Gyedal performs *'pansori'* for King Heonjong

1836

Yun Gwangyeon publishes wife's collected works in *'Jeongildang yugo'*

1861

Kim Jeongho completes *'Daedong yeojido'*

1862

Peasant uprising in Jinju

In the late eighteenth century was a man who lived just outside Hanyang, beyond the city's great eastern gate. He made his living by reading out novels, traveling to a different place each day to share stories with various gathered audiences.

The man didn't just read from a text; he filled his performance with impersonations and theatrical gestures, bringing the stories to life. Then, just when the hero or heroine was on the brink of disaster or the story had reached a climax, he would stop in his tracks. The audience, overcome with curiosity, would throw coins and beg him to finish the story. Feigning reluctance, the man would now carry on his narrative. Professional storytellers like this

A 'jeongisu' by Cheonggyecheon Stream This man, dressed up in Joseon-style clothing, is recreating the role of a *jeongisu*, or professional storyteller, by Cheonggyecheon Stream in central Seoul. A good storyteller, animating a performance with dramatic gestures and actions, can draw an audience right into the story.

were known as *jeongisu*, which roughly means "tellers of wonderful tales."

Aural fiction: Hangeul novels

Popular texts read by *jeongisu* included novels like *Simcheong jeon* ("The Tale of Simcheong"), *Sukhyang jeon* ("The Tale of Sukhyang") and *Seolingui jeon* ("The Tale of Xue Rengui"). Most of these texts were written in Hangeul rather than in classical Chinese. As they told these tales, *jeongisu* would keep an eye on the reactions of their audiences, occasionally improvising new twists and turns to the plot as they saw fit. This meant that the content of novels kept evolving.

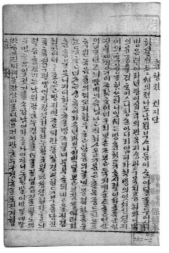 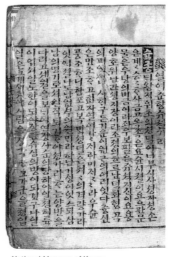

Different versions of 'Chunhyang jeon'
The authors of Hangeul novels are generally unknown. In many cases, moreover, the same novel differs from one version to the next. This is because the stories were not written from start to finish by a single author, but evolved gradually through a process of oral transmission from one storyteller to the next. These photos show two different versions of *Chunhyang jeon*: the copy on the left is known as the "Anseong edition," while that on the right is *Yeollyeo Chunhyang sujeolga* ("Song of the Faithful Lady, Chunhyang").

–National Library of Korea   –National Museum of Korea

As a result, different versions of the same novel often contain small discrepancies. Even *Chunhyang jeon* ("The Tale of Chunhyang"), one of the best-known surviving traditional tales, now exists in several versions that share the same overall plot but differ when it comes to certain details.

While some people, like the *jeongisu* I've just mentioned, recited novels in the streets, others went from one private home to another doing the same thing. Still others carried around collections of novels, selling or renting them out. They would put together bundles of the most popular works and make their way from door to door, like mobile equivalents of the book rental stores you still sometimes find in Korea today.

Women were the biggest fans of Hangeul novels. The daughters of *yangban*, wealthy merchants or professional interpreters read their way through story after story. Popular works included *Kongjui Patjui* ("Kongjui and Patjui"; a story similar to Cinderella), *Janghwa Hongnyeon jeon* ("The Tale of Janghwa and Hongnyeon"), *Sukhyang jeon* and *Hong Gildong jeon* ("The Tale of Hong Gildong"). Some of these had originally been written in classical Chinese and later translated into Korean using Hangeul; others were composed in Hangeul from the start. And some, such as *Heungbu jeon* ("The Tale of Heungbu"), *Simcheong jeon* and *Chunhyang jeon* were adaptations of famous *pansori* tales.

'Pansori' performance
A master singer performs *pansori*, accompanied by a drummer providing the beat and occasional words of encouragement. *Pan* simply denotes a specific area where an event or spectacle takes place, while *sori* means "song."

The authors of these Hangeul novels are unknown. They were primarily oral and aural tales, meant to be listened to rather than read. As they passed from one storyteller to another, their plots went on gradually shifting so that no single person could be called their author.

'Pansori' enters the 'yangban' realm

The roots of *pansori* lie in *muga*, shamanic songs popular in Korea's southwestern Jeolla-do region. Have you ever seen a shaman conducting a *gut* ritual, her songs accompanied by musicians playing drums and gongs? It's said that shamans and musicians with good voices became *pansori* singers, while those without such singing skills became the drummers that accompanied them.

As you probably know, shamans and entertainers in Joseon belonged to the ranks of *cheonmin*, the lowest social class, and were treated with the same level of contempt as slaves. *Pansori*, too, began among *cheonmin*.

Pansori entertainers traveled around, performing at busy places like markets and farming villages. As word got around that their shows were great fun to watch, however, they found themselves invited increasingly often to perform in wealthy homes. Soon, some *yangban* started performing *pansori* themselves. One example was Gwon Samdeuk, a *yangban* who earned himself a reputation as a master singer.

Just as the best singers today are idolized by young people, famous master *pansori* singers were immensely popular in

'Pansori' in the yard of a 'yangban' home
Partygoers in the yard of a wealthy household are being entertained by a *pansori* performance. The drummer is keeping time for the singer, while a crowd of onlookers has gathered beyond the wall.

Former home of Sin Jaehyo
Sin was an official in Gochang, Jeolla-do Province. A man of considerable wealth, he supported *pansori* entertainers. So great was Sin's influence that it was said to be impossible to join the ranks of master singers without getting on his good side. This photo shows the house in Gochang where he once lived.

Joseon. Influential *yangban* households often booked them to perform at parties.

Some artists were even summoned to perform before the king, and given official titles as a reward. A performer named Yeom Gyedal, for example, entertained King Heonjong and was granted the title *dongji*. Heungseon Daewongun, too, was a big fan of *pansori*, awarding official titles to master singers Park Mansun and Jeong Chunpung.

Though *pansori* began among commoners, it gradually changed as its popularity increased in *yangban* circles. The lyrics of popular works acquired more classical Chinese elements, reflecting *yangban* influence, while their themes shifted towards Neo-Confucian ethics and morals held dear by scholar-aristocrats, such as loyalty, filial piety and chastity.

A man named Sin Jaehyo was responsible for bringing *pansori* even further into the *yangban* domain. Sin arranged the various orally transmitted *pansori* tales into just six standard works and modified their content to suit *yangban* tastes. These were *Simcheong ga* ("Song of Simcheong"), *Heungbu ga* ("Song of Heungbu"), *Chunhyang ga* ("Song of Chunhyang"), *Sugung ga* ("Song of the Sea Palace"), *Jeokbyeok ga* ("Song of the Red Cliffs") and *Byeongangsoe taryeong* ("The Ballad of Byeongangsoe").

Masked dances: expressions of commoner life

While *pansori* drifted into *yangban* circles, masked dances stayed true to the world of commoners. Surviving works today include "Hahoe Tallori" of Hahoe Village in Andong, Gyeongsangbuk-do Province; "Sajanori" of Bukcheong; "Bongsan Talchum" of Hwanghae-do Province; and "Ogwangdaenori" of Tongyeong.

Masked dances are full of the thoughts and feelings of commoners. Let's look at a passage from Bongsan Talchum in which the star of the show, Malttugi, attacks a *yangban*. There's something deeply satisfying about the way Malttugi tears a strip off the preening aristocrat and his obsession with keeping up appearances:

Malttugi: Shhh! Look who's coming! It's the *yangban*! But don't be fooled: he's not exactly the "high-flying" sort of *yangban* you hear about with their scholastic factions and dazzling civil service careers! This gentlemen is certainly not prime minister material.

Yangban: Hey! Just who do you think you are?

Audiences would have laughed till their sides split as Malttugi ran rings

Bongsan Talchum
Malttugi, on the left, lays into a group of vain, self-obsessed *yangban* on the right.

● **Masks**
– Seoul National University Museum
These masks, made from dried
gourds, are used in a dance called
"Yangju Byeolsan daenori."
– National Folk Museum of Korea

Sangjwa

Nunkkeumjeogi

Meokseung

Omjung

'Kkokdugaksinorum'
This play is performed by
puppets operated by strings
from behind the scenes.
Young children love it.

around the hapless *yangban*.

So when and why did mask dances first appear? Their origins lie in the local *gut* that were held in each village to pray for a good harvest. Such ceremonies would begin with a rite, which was followed by a mask dance performance to entertain the villagers.

Other masked dances, such as the "Sandaenori," developed in cities with thriving commercial scenes. In fact, the Sandaenori was performed by specialist groups of entertainers who sometimes appeared at official state events. These included the "Naryehui," a ceremony held at the royal palace on Lunar New Year's Eve to drive away evil spirits.

Other genres of popular culture included puppet shows and "foot mask" dramas. Puppet shows, of course, starred puppets controlled by strings, while foot mask dramas were performed by people wearing masks on their feet. Performances of both genres were generally put on by troupes of traveling actors who roamed the country making a living from their talents.

Folk paintings: art of the people

Painting was one of the essential art forms that every Joseon *yangban* had to master. The men's quarters in most *yangban* homes featured a folding screen adorned with beautiful landscape scenes.

Many *yangban*, such as Gang Sehwang, Yun Duseo, Jeong Seon and Kim Jeonghui, produced outstanding paintings of their own. But such figures would never have described themselves as painters or made it their profession. For them, painting was simply another skill to be cultivated.

But there were professional artists, too. Known as court painters, they were employed by a royal office charged with producing all paintings required by the state: typically royal portraits and key scenes from a variety of ceremonies and events. Among them was Kim Hongdo, perhaps the best-known in Joseon. Court painters were not *yangban* but of *jungin* social status.

But painting, too, began to change. By late Joseon, professional painters had begun to appear among the general public. Known as commoner artists, they produced the kind of works we now know as folk paintings.

Folk paintings are not as sophisticated or refined as works by *yangban* or court painters, but the way they express the lives and feelings of the people give them a much more

Real landscape paintings and genre paintings
The most striking change in late-Joseon art was the emergence of a trend of "real landscape" paintings and genre paintings. Real landscape works offered realistic depictions of Korean nature, while genre paintings vividly illustrated the lives of commoners and *yangban* at the time.

● Folk paintings – National Folk Museum of Korea

Peonies and fantastic rocks Works such as this one, which shows peonies blooming by strangely shaped rocks, often adorned the panels of folding screens.

Tiger and magpies The tiger made frequent appearances in folk paintings as a force for driving away evil spirits.

Character pictures These images were based on Chinese characters. The one on the left is 義 (*ui*; "righteousness"), while the one on the right is 禮 (*ye*; "propriety").

familiar feel. Their subjects include tigers to chase away evil spirits, pomegranates symbolizing fertility, pictures of bookcases to encourage hard study, mandarin ducks representing marital harmony…

Folk paintings provide honest testimony to the desires of Joseon commoners to have many children and live happily together, with plenty to eat. Perhaps this is why they are usually full of bright colors, rather than dark or somber.

Commoner artists left their works unsigned. Why? Despite their talent, they led lives of poverty. They would make their ways around markets and other crowded places, painting pictures to order in return for something to eat and a bed for the night. Maybe this was why they chose not to leave their names on their works.

Folk paintings were generally bought by well-off commoners. Though they needed something to decorate their homes, they couldn't afford the kind of refined works enjoyed by *yangban* and settled instead for folk art, which they hung on their walls or stood in their rooms as folding screens.

Popular culture: the product of social change

Popular culture began appearing in the eighteenth century for several reasons. Mask dances offer a good illustration of the weakening social caste system and the circumstances of fallen *yangban* in this period. More and more people were using money to buy themselves *yangban* status, with farmers and *jungin* who had managed to save up some cash desperate to become *yangban* at all costs. Why? Partly because they were fed up of being looked down upon, but mostly because they wanted to enjoy tax exempt status. *Yangban*, as I've already mentioned, didn't have to pay taxes to the state.

At the time, the state was selling *yangban* certificates in exchange for money or rice in an attempt to make much-needed cash. Such certificates were known as *gongmyeongcheop* or *napsokchaek*.

While some commoners were becoming

A 'gongmyeongcheop'
The term *gongmyeong* indicated that the space for a name on these certificates had been left blank, as you can see in the photo below. This was effectively a certificate that granted *yangban* status to whoever bought it and wrote his name in the blank space. People bought *gongmyeongcheop* because *yangban* status brought tax exemption.
– Samcheok Municipal Museum

'Chunhyangjeondo'
This Joseon-period work
shows a meeting between
Chunhyang and her lover,
Mongnyong, who has
become a royal inspector.
– Central Museum of Kyunghee
University

yangban by buying the necessary papers, large numbers of existing *yangban* had fallen on hard times, retaining their statuses in the most nominal way and living effectively the same lives as farmers. This was due to the large gap between Hanyang-based *yangban* who held actual government positions, and their unemployed counterparts in the provinces.

The total number of *yangban* was now higher than before, but their authority was at an all-time low. There was also a growing number of *yangban* who shirked the traditional responsibilities and duties associated with their elevated status and were content with simply putting on airs. Commoners now began secretly making fun of aristocrats. The scene in the Bongsan Talchum where Malttugi shows such contempt for the *yangban* before him is a direct expression of this phenomenon.

Changes in the social class system are also reflected in *Chunhyang jeon*, which tells the tale of how Chunhyang, the daughter of a *gisaeng*, and Yi Mongryong, the son of a *yangban* family, use the power of love to break through class barriers. In the novel, Chunhyang becomes the official wife of Mongryong once he has been appointed an undercover royal inspector, and is even granted the title "Lady of Virtue" by the king himself. In reality, however, this would have been impossible: no daughter of a *gisaeng*, born into *cheonmin* status, could ever have become the official wife of a *yangban*. A concubine, maybe. In any case, commoners had succeeded in boldly bringing down the high wall of social division, if only in a work of fiction.

Now, hopefully, it will be clearer to you why popular culture was the product of various social changes at this time.

 'Samulnori'

Samulnori, the term that has now become synonymous with traditional music, was in fact born in 1978 as the name of a band that played it. The genre uses four instruments (*samul*): the *kkwaenggwari* (small gong), the *jing* (larger gong), *janggu* (hourglass drum) and *buk* (barrel drum).

But *samul* was originally a Buddihst word that refers to the four instruments played at the beginning of a Buddhist service: the *beopgo* (large, hanging drum), *unpan* (cloud-shaped gong), *mogeo* (hollow wooden fish) and *beomjong* (large bronze bell).

Suddenly, not long ago, *samul* came to refer to the *kkwaenggwari*, *jing*, *janggu* and *buk* instead of the Buddhist quartet.

Before the term *samulnori* was coined, traditional music was referred to as *nongak* or *pungmul*.

'Mogeo' and 'beopgo'
Samul was originally a Buddhist word. This image shows two of the four Buddhist *samul* instruments: the *mogeo*, a wooden fish, and the *beopgo*, a drum.

?!

Yi Danjeon, the 'nobi' poet

In Joseon, poetry was the preserve of the upper classes. Peasants plowing the fields and village women knew neither how to read it nor to write it. At this time, poetry was written in classical Chinese. There was one *nobi*, however, who knew how to write in this difficult literary language. His name was Yi Danjeon and he worked in the home of the Yu family at the time of King Jeongjo.

Yi took an interest in writing from a young age. When the sons of the Yu household were studying, he would secretly listen in on their lessons to learn for himself. He would work by day and stay up writing poetry by candlelight at night. Yi would then take his poems to famous poets and scholars and ask for their opinions. He even went to study with the Yi Deongmu, the famous Silhak scholar and poet. Some ten years later, the standard of his work was recognized by several *yangban*.

But Yi was continuously despised by most aristocrats, who found it outrageous that a low-born *nobi* was writing poetry. Moreover, he is said to have been very ugly: a short figure with one eye and a pockmarked face. And he wasn't much of a talker. Yi, however, remained undaunted and pressed on resolutely with his writing. Still, it seems there were times when he lamented the state of his existence. Here's one of his poems:

What must the Creator have been thinking
When he brought me into existence here,
in a corner of Joseon?
By nature, I'm a cross between a fool and
an idiot.
By appearance, I'm half-skinny, half-lanky.
All my friends are *yangban*
but I'm another man's servant.
If I ever happen to make it up to Heaven
I'll ask Buddha what my strange fate on this
earth meant.

After overcoming immense social obstacles to
become a poet, Yi died suddenly at the age of
just thirty-six.

'Chwihu ganhwa'
('Drinking Wine and Admiring the Flowers')
This painting by late-Joseon painter Kim Hongdo shows two
men chatting in a beautiful setting, with playing cranes and a
blossoming plum tree. What must the *nobi* here be thinking
as he prepares tea under a nearby tree? Yi Danjeon, the poet-
nobi, would surely have understood how he felt.

CHAPTER 5

Love and marriage in Joseon

Yu Huichun and his wife, Yi Eungtae and his wife, and Sin Saimdang and her husband all lived according to the old Korean tradition. There was nothing strange about Yu's wife sitting down with him to enjoy the wine sent by the king and write him a cheerful poem or two. And it was perfectly natural when Yi's wife lay next to her husband, wondering if other couples loved each other as much as they did.

TIME
LINE —————— 1776 ——————— 1780 ——————— 1791 ——————————

Joseon period   Park Jiwon travels to Qing;   'Keumnanjeongwon'
Jeongjo takes throne;   writes 'Yeolha ilgi'   abolished except
builds Gyujanggak   for Yuguijeon

Many young Korean women today count themselves lucky not to have lived in Joseon. Life as a daughter-in-law was notoriously hard. The husband's status in relation to his wife was something akin to a god. Married life was no fun, and women weren't even allowed to visit their own families at will.

Even in the home, gender segregation kept men and women apart, in their respective quarters. The husband would take no interest in managing the household, while the wife would never ask about what business her other half got up to outside the home. Couples were as distant as strangers, and wives had to put up with everything that came their way through a combination of submission and patience.

Women's lives were constrained by Confucian ethics such as "couple distinctions," the "three-fold path of obedience," the "seven transgressions," and "once married, forever a stranger."

Couple distinctions held that a husband and wife must observe separate, non-overlapping duties.

The three-fold path of obedience stated that a woman must obey her father in youth, her husband in marriage, and her son in old age.

The seven transgressions were offenses for which a wife could be thrown out by her husband's family, and included lack of piety towards parents-in-law, failure to bear a son, jealousy, serious illness and so on.

Once married, forever a stranger indicated that a woman was no longer considered part of her own family after her wedding.

Today, though, I'd like to describe something a little different from the conventioual picture. Have a read and see what you think.

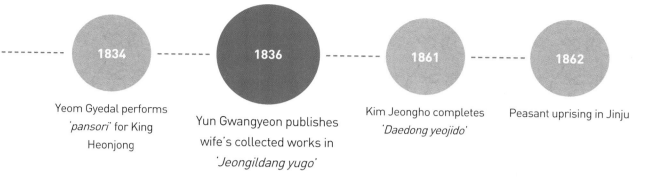

1834

Yeom Gyedal performs *'pansori'* for King Heonjong

1836

Yun Gwangyeon publishes wife's collected works in *'Jeongildang yugo'*

1861

Kim Jeongho completes *'Daedong yeojido'*

1862

Peasant uprising in Jinju

Yu Huichun was an official who lived in the 16th century, at the time of King Seonjo. A talented writer with an excellent memory and a strong spirit, he became a favorite of the king. Yu kept a regular diary, which contains several of the conversations and poems he exchanged with his wife.

One winter's day, while snow was falling outside, Yu and his wife enjoyed a pear and

'Hoehollyedo' This painting shows a *hoehollye*, a ceremony held to celebrate a sixtieth wedding anniversary. At the *hoehollye*, the elderly husband and wife would put on wedding garments again and hold another wedding ceremony. Since the average life expectancy in Joseon was short, a *hoehollye* was a very rare event. The elderly man and woman look delighted as their children, grandchildren and relatives gather round to congratulate them.
–National Museum of Korea

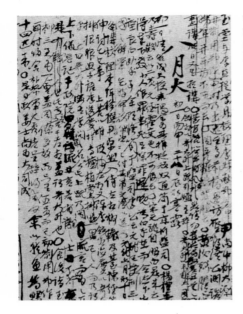

Yu Huichun's diary
Written in classical Chinese, Yu's diary contains several entries recording conversations and poems exchanged with his wife. She, well aware of her husband's work, cooperates with him, while Yu shares many confidences with her.

some wine that he had received as gifts from the king. He wrote in his diary:

My wife and I shared a fine pear from the palace. It was of the best quality: not dry but full of juice. The wine, too, was wonderful. We kept on remarking to each other how good it was. My wife wrote me a poem:

On a snowy day like this
it's hard enough to get hold of any wine
let alone a bottle of wonderful golden liquor
sent as a gift from the palace.

At the first sip
my face blushes crimson.
I drift back to earlier, carefree days,
as we enjoy ourselves together.

Do other couples love each other like us?

The picture that emerges of Yu and his wife through the diary differs considerably to the conventional image we have of married life in Joseon. The wife knows all about her husband's work and helps him actively with it, while he in turn trusts her and shares many confidences. Their respect and love for each other seem even more reliable and serious than the relationship between many couples today. But, you say, surely Yu and his wife were an exception to the rule? Let's look at another example, then.

In 1998, builders digging foundations for a house at the foot of a mountain in Andong, Gyeongsangbuk-do, came across a tomb. On the chest of its occupant was a sheet of paper, which researchers carefully removed. Written in close handwriting on the paper was a letter that read as follows:

"My dear husband,

You always used to tell me we would grow old and gray-haired together, then die side by side. How could you leave me behind like this?······ When we lay down together, I would ask you: 'Darling, do you think other couples love each other as much as we do? Can they really be like us?' How could you forget everything I said, and move on without me? There's no way I can go on living without you. I want to be with you as soon as

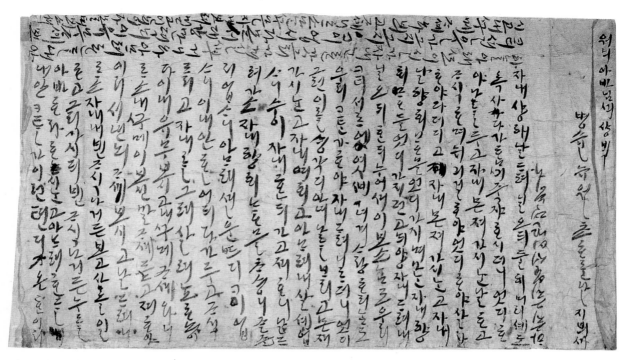

Letter from Yi Eungtae's wife
This letter was written to Yi, in Hangeul, by his wife. It gives no indication of her name or age.
–Andong National University Museum

possible…"

This was the tomb of Yi Eungtae, a man who died over 400 years ago, in 1586, at the age of just thirty-one. Yi was an Andong *yangban* whose sudden death left behind his wife and young son, Won. His wife, in her sadness, had written a letter to be buried with him.

The kind of marital love contained in this letter seems far more honest and powerful than anything we know today.

So what's going on? Why are these Joseon women who, we imagined, would barely ever see their husband's faces, let alone express their love for them, suddenly sitting down opposite their husbands, exchanging poems and talking freely about their emotions?

When did gender discrimination begin?

Much of our conventional image of Joseon women is either wrong or exaggerated. In fact, they weren't subject to much discrimination—until around the seventeenth century, at least. We can infer this by looking at customs related to property inheritance and ancestral rites.

Until the mid-Joseon period, property was divided equally among sons and daughters. Even after marriage, women would receive their share of inheritance from their original families.

Ancestral rites, too, were naturally held by married daughters and their husbands if a family had no sons. And the children of some families would take it in turns to

Yi family inheritance document
Documents like this one were used to record the division of property such as land, *nobi* and homes among children as part of inheritance. This photo is of an inheritance document detailing the division of assets among Yi Yulgok and his brothers and sisters. Until the mid-Joseon period, property was divided equally among sons and daughters.
–Konkuk University Museum

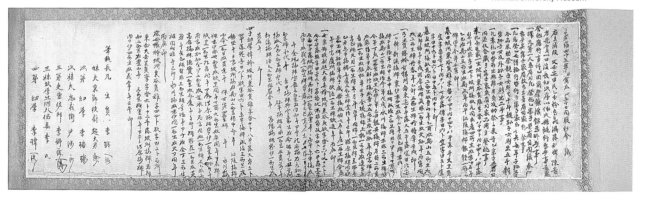

Wedding day
This genre painting by late-Joseon painter Kim Jungeun shows a groom on horseback making his way to the house of his bride.

conduct such rites even if there was an eldest son. There was no discrimination between grandsons born to sons and those born to daughters, either: it was not unusual for the latter to conduct ancestral rites. No family without its own son adopted one to avoid severance of the ancestral line. And many women re-married if their husbands died.

These non-discriminatory systems of property inheritance and ancestral rites were intimately linked to marriage customs at the time. The common view today is that marriage for a Joseon woman meant living only with her in-laws and sacrificing herself entirely for them. In fact, however, exactly the opposite was the case in early Joseon. Women normally stayed with their own families after getting married.

The custom of husbands going to live in the homes of their brides, raising children there and only returning to their own households with their families once the children had grown up a fair bit was an old one that lasted from the Three Kingdoms period, through Goryeo and well into early Joseon. This long-lasting tradition left an imprint that remains even in contemporary Korean language: the term *jangga gada*, meaning, for a man, "to get married," literally describes going to live in the home of his father-in-law.

Figures such as Kim Jongjik, the scholar esteemed as the father of the *sarim* faction, and Jo Sik, the great Neo-Confucian thinker and peer of Yi Hwang, both grew up in the family homes of their mothers and went to live in those of their wives after getting married. Yulgok Yi I, too, was born into and grew up with his mother's family and conducted rites for its ancestors. If even leading Neo-Confucian scholars still followed this age-old tradition, it goes without saying that the general public must have done the same.

Let's look at the case of Sin Saimdang. Sin was a wonderful mother who raised the great scholar Yulgok Yi I, a wise wife who always kept her husband on the right path, and a dutiful daughter-in-law who took good care of her parents-in-law. Not only that: she also worked hard to cultivate her own talents, becoming one of the few female Joseon poets and painters widely known today. Effectively, she was

'Chochungdo'
painting by Sin Saimdang
Sin was a particularly talented artist. This painting, which belongs to the *chochungdo* ("plants and insects") genre, was featured on a folding screen.

Wooden geese (right) and nuptial cups (below)
At a Joseon wedding, the groom would take a wild goose to the house of his bride, place it on a table and bow down before it. Called the *jeonallye*, this ceremony was performed to symbolize the exceptionally strong love between pairs of wild geese. Originally, a live wild goose was used for the ceremony, but this was replaced with a wooden substitute for the sake of practicality. Nuptial cups, made from dried gourds, are used by the bride and groom to drink nuptial wine.
– National Folk Museum of Korea

superwoman.

When you look again at Sin's life, one or two other facts emerge. She was raised in the household of her mother, in the eastern coastal city of Gangneung, then married Yi Wonsu at the age of nineteen. After her wedding, she carried on living with her own family. Is that because she was an only daughter? Not at all: she was the second of five sisters.

Sin bore and raised three daughters and four sons in her family home, including Yulgok Yi I. It was only some twenty years after getting married that she finally left her own family and went to live with her in-laws in Hanyang. She was now thirty-eight years old. Sin died ten years after this, which means she spent the majority of her life in her own family home. Her story is an excellent illustration of the enduring custom of husbands going to live with the families of their wives.

So when did things change? The practice of women moving in with their in-laws gradually began replacing the opposite arrangement around the seventeenth century. It originated in China, where grooms took their brides into their own homes for the wedding ceremony and stayed there afterwards.

A characteristic of the Chinese system was that marriage put

A bride on the way to her groom's house
This palanquin is on its way to the house of the groom. What kind of expression might we find on the face of the bride inside?

the groom, his parents and his relatives at the center of the bride's life, while distancing her from her own family. As far as the latter was concerned, then, the once married, always a stranger principle now applied. But the Korean custom had the opposite effect, placing the husband at the center of his wife's family. From the bride's point of view, life carried on much as before and her status in the household was far from inferior to that of her husband. No one favored sons over daughters or husbands over wives.

Yu Huichun and his wife, Yi Eungtae and his wife, and Sin Saimdang and her husband all lived according to the old Korean tradition. There was nothing strange about Yu's wife sitting down with him to enjoy the wine sent by the king and write him a cheerful poem or two. And it was perfectly natural when Yi's wife lay next to her husband, wondering if other couples loved each other as much as they did.

Sin Saimdang, meanwhile, was able to become the superwoman she was thanks both to her outstanding natural talent and to the conditions that allowed it to flourish. In other words, the social climate of her time did not discriminate against women.

Changing customs

A bride on her wedding day
An immaculately made-up bride kneels down modestly at her wedding. This painting is by Elizabeth Keith, a British artist who visited Korea 100 years ago. We now think of a "traditional-style wedding" as one where the ceremony takes place at the bride's home, after which the couple move to the groom's house.

From the beginning of the Joseon period, the ruling class worked hard to alter the country's marriage customs and bring them into conformity with those of China and with Neo-Confucianism. But such deep-rooted traditions did not change overnight. Even leading Neo-Confucian scholars, not to mention everyone else, stuck with the old ways.

It took more than 200 years for a shift to the Chinese marriage custom to finally take place. People at last began to accept the new arrangement around the seventeenth century.

Korean weddings did not become exactly like

those of China, however. A new, hybrid wedding developed, in which the ceremony took place at the bride's home and the couple then went to live with the groom's family.

It wasn't just marriage customs that shifted around the seventeenth century: inheritance customs also underwent change. Where sons and daughters had once received equal shares, they now received more and less, respectively. Eldest sons, in particular, stood to inherit the most. Daughters no longer conducted ancestral rites, while among sons it was to the eldest, again, that this responsibility now generally fell.

What was the reason for these changes? It was now that the tenets of Neo-Confucianism, previously observed only by the ruling minority, had begun to spread widely among the rest of the population. There were economic reasons, too: it was believed that concentrating family wealth into the hands of just one or two children, rather than spreading it evenly, was a better way of maintaining and increasing it.

Im Yunjidang: A female Confucian scholar

"Oh, I may be a woman, but there's no difference between men and women when it comes to nature bestowed by heaven!"

So wrote Im Yunjidang, who lived in Joseon in the eighteenth century. At a time when the spread of Neo-

'Dangho' names
"Saimdang" was not Sin Saimdang's actual name. Just as many Joseon men had pen names, called *ho* in Korean, some women had *dangho* names. Examples include Sin Saimdang and Im Yunjidang.

Confucian ethics was leading to increasing discrimination against women, Im's claim that men and women were the same in terms of basic nature and merely faced different circumstances in reality was very brave.

Im was a female philosopher who had studied Neo-Confucianism in depth. She first took interest in this system of thought thanks to her home environment. Im's family turned out several Neo-Confucian scholars; one of her elder brothers, Seongju, was among the leading Neo-Confucian thinkers of the late Joseon period. From the age of around nine, Im Yunjidang began studying alongside her brothers. Together, they read and discussed books on philosophy and

 Maintaining strong identities as women

It's commonly believed that women in Joseon were not taught to write, but this is not true. Daughters in *yangban* households were taught both Hangeul and classical Chinese from a young age, and were able to read books and write poetry in the latter.

Lady Kim of Hoyeonjae wrote many poems and other works in classical Chinese. Among them was a piece called *Jagyeongmun* ("Text for Self-Enlightenment"), which contains a passage on married couples:

"Every day, I work to become more virtuous and improve myself. How shameful it would be to lose my strong identity as a woman by thinking only of my husband's approval and wellbeing!"

Kim is saying it is a shameful thing when a woman relies excessively on her husband and loses sight of her own standards. Her brimming confidence is reminiscent of what we might call a strong-minded, modern woman.

history.

When she was nineteen years old, Im married a man named Sin Gwangyu. Only eight years later, however, her husband died and she was left a widow. The couple had one child but it, too, died young.

Im Yunjidang's life conforms exactly to our image of a Joseon woman. Widowed at the young age of twenty-seven, she never remarried, remaining chaste and alone until her death, without even a child to love, in the family of her late husband. In fact, there was an unusually high number of widows in the Sin household. Im's mother-in-law had lost her husband at the age of thirty-seven, while Im's daughter-in-law was widowed at the age of just thirty when her husband, adopted to preserve the Sin family line, met an early end.

Im overcame her loneliness and pain by studying Neo-Confucianism. Perhaps the most important reason for her deep concentration on scholarship was the need to heal her mind. Ultimately, she reached the conclusion that there was no innate difference between the natures of men and women.

What would have become of Im if she was born just a little earlier, in the time of Sin Saimdang, allowing her to develop her talents to the full?

'Yunjidang yugo' ('Works of the Late Im Yunjidang') This book is a compilation of the writings of Im Yunjidang. It was published after her death, in 1796, by her younger brother Jeongju.

Gang Jeongildang and Yun Gwangyeon in love

Remember how I said how the lives of women changed a lot from the seventeenth century onwards? The spread of Neo-Confucianism led to greater emphasis on submissiveness and chastity among women. What about married couples, then? Let's have a look at the case of Gang Jeongildang and her husband, Yun Gwangyeon.

Gang and Yun got married at the end of the eighteenth century. They were both born into *yangban* families but Yun, who was not wealthy, opened a *seodang* (village school) and taught local children, while Gang brought in a bit of income by doing sewing jobs.

Even while struggling to make ends meet, Gang took every available opportunity to study. When her husband opened a book and read out loud from it, she would sit next to him and memorize the content while she sewed. She often wrote letters to him, too, in classical Chinese:

'Jeongildang yugo' ('Works of the Late Gang Jeongildang')
This book is an anthology of poetry and prose by Gang Jeongildang. She was an outstanding writer in both genres and had beautiful handwriting, too.
–Jongyeonggak, Sungkyunkwan University

"I haven't had any rice to cook for three days now. One of your students brought me a few fist-sized pumpkins on a vine. I cut them up and made a soup. I wanted to find you some wine, even just a cupful, but I couldn't get any. It makes me so sad that all I have to give you is soup…"

Gang wrote this to her husband while cooking him a soup of pumpkins, acquired with much difficulty, in a lean year when she had had no rice to cook for the previous three days. The letter is infused with her simple love for her husband. She also tells him not to slacken in his studies, even though times are hard, warning him sharply to correct his bad attitude. What did Yun think of his wife? When she died from an illness at the age of sixty-one, he wrote the following while mourning her:

"Who will answer my questions? Who will help me with the things I want to do? Who will correct me when I'm wrong?...... Now that you've abandoned me, I'm like an unmoored ship, or a blind man with no one to guide him. I sway and collapse, stumble and fall. The future looks bleak and I've nowhere to go."

Gang and Yun were both close friends and a loving couple with plenty of mutual respect. So it turns out married life in Joseon was quite different to most of the stereotypes we encounter today.

CHAPTER 6

Kim Jeongho
and 'Daedong yeojido'

"Maps show the state of the world, while geographical texts provide knowledge of all historical systems and culture," Kim Jeongho wrote in his preface to *Dongyeodoji* "These truly constitute a grand framework for governing the country."

To Kim, maps and geographical texts went hand in hand and were indispensable tools of national government. That's why he devoted his whole life to studying them.

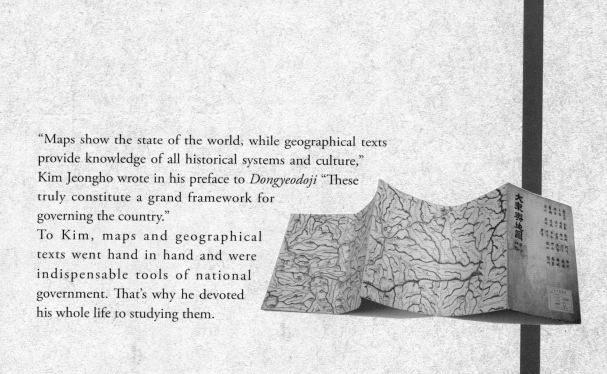

TIME LINE

1776

Joseon period
Jeongjo takes throne;
builds Gyujanggak

1780

Park Jiwon travels to Qing;
writes *Yeolha ilgi*

1791

'Keumnanjeongwon'
abolished except
for Yuguijeon

"How could anyone have made such an accurate map so long ago?"

This may be your first thought when you read about Daedong yeojido *("Detailed Map of Korea"), the famous map of the Korean Peninsula.*

Daedong yeojido *was produced some 140 years ago by a man named Kim Jeongho. Even so, it can hold its own against any map made today using the latest science and technology. An amazing feat, to be sure.*

Rumors about Kim abound: that he climbed Mt. Baekdusan eight times; that he traveled the length and the breadth of the country three times before completing the great map; that he donated it to the state, but was thrown into prison for leaking secrets, and died there; that Daedong yeojido *was seized and burned.*

And yet, the supposedly incinerated map clearly survives in good condition today. How on earth did that happen?

It turns out that quite a few other commonly accepted facts about Kim Jeongho are false, too.

Today, let's see how he really produced Daedong yeojido.

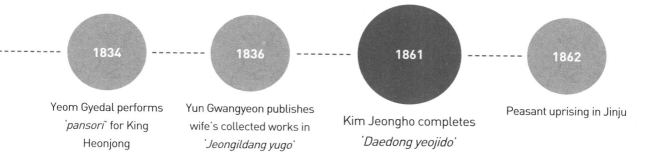

1834

1836

1861

1862

Yeom Gyedal performs *pansori* for King Heonjong

Yun Gwangyeon publishes wife's collected works in *Jeongildang yugo*

Kim Jeongho completes *Daedong yeojido*

Peasant uprising in Jinju

Who was Kim Jeongho? We don't know for certain when he was born, how he died or what kind of social background he came from. Scholars have estimated that he was born in 1804 and died in 1866, though. Some believe he was a commoner by birth; others that he was of *jungin* status or a fallen *yangban*.

The reason Kim's biography is so full of question marks is the lack of surviving records about him. We have hardly anything written about Kim by those who knew him, let alone by the man himself. Only three records remain: something written by Silhak scholar Choe Hangi, a friend of Kim; a brief mention in a book called *Ihyanggyeon mullok* ("Village

Kim Jeongho
Kim was born in Hwanghae-do Province and lived in Hanyang. It seems his family was very poor. Though he is often said to have lived only with his daughter, this is wrong: he also had a wife and son. Kim was deeply interested in geography and maps from a young age.
– National Geographic Information Institute

Observations"); and the preface to a map by Sin Heon called *Daedongbangyeodo* ("Map of Korea").

Choe Hangi left the following record of Kim in his preface to Cheonggudo:

"My friend Kim Jeongho was interested in maps from childhood. He spent much of his time looking for various materials and studied all mapmaking methods in detail. Whenever he had a moment's spare time, he would spend it on study and discussion."

Maps: a grand framework for governing the country

Kim's name generally conjures only thoughts of *Daedong yeojido*. In fact, though, he produced three other maps and three geographical texts. His other maps include two more of the whole of Joseon, *Cheonggudo* and *Dongyeodo*, and one of Hanyang, *Suseonjeondo*, while the three books are titled *Dongyeodoji*, *Yeodobiji* and *Daedongjiji*.

Kim wrote the three geographical texts before producing his maps. Such texts, known in Korean as *jiriji*, or *jiji*, brought together all kinds of information about a specific area: geography, history, industry, transport, population and so on. Kim believed that a map was the ideal way to visually represent all the information contained in a geographical text.

"Maps show the state of the world, while geographical texts

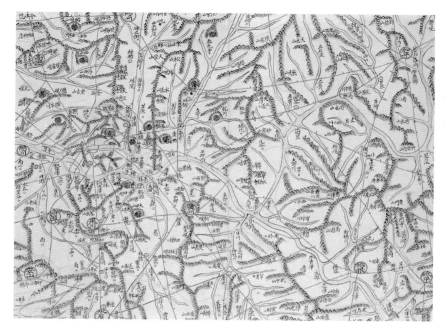

provide knowledge of all historical systems and culture," Kim wrote in his preface to *Dongyeodoji*. "These truly constitute a grand framework for governing the country."

To Kim, maps and geographical texts went hand in hand and were indispensable tools of national government. That's why he devoted his whole life to studying them.

Did Kim Jeongho really spend his time traveling around Joseon?

Kim is said to have climbed Mt. Baekdusan eight times and traveled around the country three times in order to create *Daedong yeojido*. I remember reading this claim in his biography when I was young. I felt sorry for him, battling

! What is the Baekdudaegan Range?

"Taebaeksanmaek" and "Sobaeksanmaek," terms familiar to us today, did not exist in Joseon. Taebaeksanmaek and various other mountain names we use now were first coined in 1903 by a Japanese geologist named Koto Bunjiro and went on to survive through the colonial period. Place names used for mountain ranges in Joseon referred to *daegan*, *jeonggan* and *jeongmaek*—Baekdudaegan, Jangbaekjeonggan and Nangnamjeongmaek, for example.

So what is the difference between the words *sanmaek* and *daegan*? The former refers more to geological structures in the ground itself, while the latter is based on the forms of mountains as they emerge above the ground. The maps we use today show us geological features in the ground. This is why we sometimes follow a map to where there should be a mountain, but find that it's not there. In Korea, the geology of the earth's crust and the actual appearance of mountains above the ground is not always the same, since the country's mountain ranges are so old.

'Dongguk daejeondo ("Large Complete Map of Korea"),' with the Baekdudaegan Range clearly visible The Baekdudaegan Range runs all the way down from Mt. Baekdusan to Mt. Jirisan. Other ranges branch out from it at several points along the way. The Joseon geographical text *Sangyeongpyo* ("Chart of Mountain Ranges") divides these ranges into the Baedudaegan, the Jangbaekjeonggan and thirteen *jeongmaek*. –National Museum of Korea hunger and thirst and wearing his way through multiple pairs of straw shoes as he trudged the length and breadth of the land.

This story, however, isn't true. It was made up later on. *Daedong yeojido* was not made by anyone traveling across the country and taking direct measurements; rather, it was a grand synthesis of many existing maps.

Of course, Kim probably visited certain areas when he found discrepancies between the maps he was comparing, or if he found something suspicious. But given the state of transport at the time, Kim's own humble means and the quantity and quality of his work, is seems to me there's no way he could have made three tours of the country and climbed its faraway highest mountain eight times.

There was no need to make new surveys when compiling a map. Jeong Sanggi, a scholar who lived before Kim, had produced *Dongguk jido*, the most accurate map of its time. But even *Dongguk jido* was produced through a synthesis of the maps handed down through Jeong's family and others, rather than by surveying the land directly. After all, even the renowned French cartographer, Jean-Baptiste Bourguignon

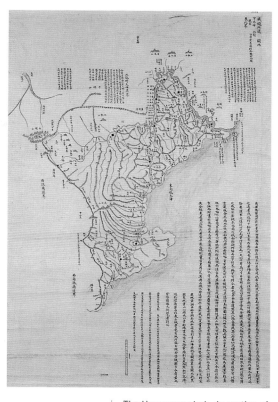

The Hamgyeongbuk-do section of Jeong Sanggi's 'Dongguk jido'
Jeong Sanggi was born some 100 years before Kim Jeongho. He produced *Dongguk jido*, the map of Korea most widely used until the publication of *Daedong yeojido*. Jeong, who suffered from poor health, gave up studying for the state examination and devoted himself to researching Korean geography and maps.
– Kyujanggak Institute for Korean Studies

Kim Jeongho working on 'Daedong yeojido'
Kim's masterpiece was made by consulting and synthesizing a wide range of existing maps.

'Daedong yeojido'
This remarkable map is made from twenty-two separate, foldable booklets that measure 3.3 meters in width and 6.3 in height when all brought together: as high as a three-story building. Each of its individual booklets, however, is as small and portable as a normal book when folded. This made it highly convenient for users, who could carry around particular parts of the map as and when needed.

d'Anville, had produced the most accurate world map of this era without setting foot outside his own country.

It's tempting to assume that not a single accurate map of Joseon existed before *Daedong yeojido*. In fact, however, the opposite was true. Maps were highly important in a variety of fields, including politics, economics and military affairs, and Koreans had been making them for a long time by then - since the Three Kingdoms period, in fact.

Goguryeo kept maps of its entire territory, while Baekje had a map called *Dojeok* ("Map"). In Goryeo, meanwhile, a map of the country called *Jirido* ("Geographical Map") was produced. A Goryeo man by the name of Na Hongyu became famous for his maps of Goryeo and China. Unfortunately, however, not a singe map from the Three Kingdoms or Goryeo period survives today. Looking at Joseon maps does give us some idea of the techniques applied to their predecessors, however.

Joseon scholars produced a wide variety of maps, with some depicting the entire country and others focusing only on certain counties or smaller administrative areas. There was a map of the world, too: called *Honil gangni yeokdae gukdo ji do*, it was based on a Yuan world map. A handmade copy is housed at a university library in Kyoto, Japan.

A map can't be made overnight. Only those who have spent years building up the necessary mapmaking skills and geographical knowledge are up to the task. *Daedong yeojido* was not just the product of Kim Jeongho's talent and effort. It was the culmination of a long process; a synthesis of all the geography and mapmaking techniques that had developed

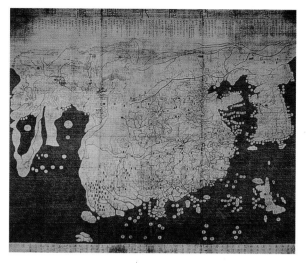

'Honil gangni yeokdae gukdo jido' ('Map of Integrated Lands and Regions of Historical Countries and Capitals')
Though the Korean Peninsula appears disproportionately large in this map, its outline is pretty accurate. Japan is depicted as a very small country to the south of Korea. These proportions give us some idea of how people at the time thought China and Joseon to be the center of the world.
–National Museum of Korea

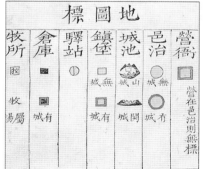

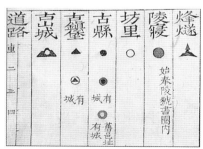

Legend from 'Daedong yeojido'
Kim's giant map used a legend to assign symbols to features such as relay posts and warehouses. These symbols were then used on the actual map, as a form of visual abbreviation. This made the map simpler, easier to read, and able to hold more information.
–Kyujanggak Institute for Korean Studies

in Korea over the past millennium, from the Three Kingdoms period onwards. Now, hopefully, you know how wrong it is to claim that there were no decent maps of Korea before *Daedong yeojido*.

Daedong yeojido contained information essential for everyday life. Rivers were marked with curves and roads with straight lines, with distances marked using a dot every ten *ri*. Navigable and non-navigable rivers were distinguished by the use of double and single lines, respectively.

Korea was divided into twenty-two gradations from north to south and nineteen from east to west, with one section of the map depicting each division. Known as "sectional maps," these are very convenient because they negate the need to mark scale in other ways.

Was 'Daedong yeojido' really burned?

Yet another rumor about *Daedong yeojido* claims that when Kim finally completed his life's masterpiece and offered it to Heungseon Daewongun, Korea's regent at the time, he was arrested for revealing important national secrets without permission. Kim and his daughter, this story goes, were thrown into prison and died there, while the map itself was incinerated. This is not true, either.

Some of the woodblocks for the supposedly burned map

Map section and woodblock
Like the *Tripitaka Koreana*, *Daedong yeojido* was carved onto woodblocks, allowing as many copies as were needed to be printed. This enabled large numbers of people to obtain copies and eliminated the risk of inaccuracy that came with reproduction by hand.
–National Museum of Korea

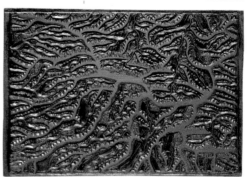

appeared in public in 1931, as part of an exhibition at Keijo Imperial University. Indeed, the *Daedong yeojido* woodblocks survive even today. One is housed in the Korean Christian Museum at Soongsil University, while eleven more are in the collection of the National Museum of Korea. Which proves that the story about the Daewongun confiscating the map is a lie.

Neither is there a shred of evidence to back up the claim that Kim died in prison for disclosing state secrets. More than anything, making maps without government permission was not illegal.

Kim produced *Daedong yeojido* at a time when plenty of other civilians were making maps. Jeong Sanggi's *Dongguk jido* and Yun Duseo's *Dongguk yeojijido* are just two prominent examples. So there was nothing unusual about the production of *Daedong yeojido* and it certainly wasn't a crime of any sort, let alone anything as serious as revealing national secrets.

Choe Hangi's 'Jigu jeonhu do' ('Map of the Front and Back of the Earth')
Choe was a childhood friend of Kim. These photos are of *Jigu jeonhu do*, a map he produced showing the "front" (right) and "back" (left) sides of the earth. Choe drew the map with Kim's help.
–Kyujanggak Institute for Korean Studies

Moreover, a record would remain if Kim had died in prison for such a crime against the state but nothing of the sort exists.

Claims that Kim produced the famous map entirely on his own are also off the mark. He had several supporters, including military officer Choe Seonghwan, former minister of defense Sin Heon, and his friend, the Silhak scholar Choe Hangi. These men helped Kim cover the expenses of his project and collect the necessary materials and information. Sin was the man who represented Joseon when the Treaty of Ganghwa was signed with Japan. He probably helped gain access for Kim to various materials kept deep in royal palace archives.

The 'story of Kim Jeongho' as told in the Japanese colonial period

So what is the origin of the story about the Daewongun throwing Kim into prison for leaking state secrets? It appears in *Joseoneo dokbon* ("A Korean Reader"), a text published by the Japanese colonial government that was roughly equivalent to what we could call an elementary school textbook. This same book contains the claims that Kim made three tours of the country and climbed Mt. Baekdusan eight times. Let's take a look at what Lesson 4 in Volume V of *Joseoneo dokbon* has to say about Kim Jeongho:

"After ten years, [Kim] finally completed the famous *Daedeong yeojido*. During this time, he is said to have traveled all eight provinces of Korea three times and climbed Mt. Baekdusan eight times. ... He presented the map to the Daewongun. But the regent, as everybody knows, had strong anti-foreign feelings. When he saw the map, he was furious, saying, 'Leaking state secrets to other countries without permission in this way is a very serious crime.'

He seized the woodblocks of the map and threw Jeongho and his daughter into prison. Seemingly unable to endure the pain of prison life, they died, full of bitterness, in short succession. ... When the Russo-Japanese War began, *Daedong yeojido* proved enormously helpful to our [Japan's] military. Later, moreover, it proved unmatched as a source of information in the [Japanese] Government-General's land survey. Anyone who sees it is amazed by its detail and its accuracy. In the end, Kim's many troubles bore magnificent fruit."

In fact, somebody else had already told a similar story about Kim before *Joseoneo dokbon* was published. This was none other than Choe Namseon, the man who drafted the Korean Declaration of Independence at the time of the March

1 Movement in 1919. Writing about Kim and his map, largely forgotten at the time, in the daily *Dong-A ilbo* newspaper and the magazine *Byeolgeongon* ("Another World"), Choe claimed that Kim had made his way round the country as part of his mapmaking project, and that he had died in prison.

Later, Kim was featured in other magazines such as *Haksaeng* ("Student") and *Eorini* ("Youngster"), too. Nonetheless, it was because of *Joseoneo dokbon* that his "story" became widely spread.

Choe Namseon's motive in writing about Kim Jeongho was to bring the cartographer and his map, which had slipped into obscurity, back to wide attention and create awareness of their value. So why did the colonial government include the story in *Joseoneo dokbon*? There was a hidden motive at work here. After making Korea its colony, Japan created a body called the Government-General to run the country. School textbooks, like many other things, had to follow the policies of the colonial occupier. I believe the Japanese authorities included the story of Kim and

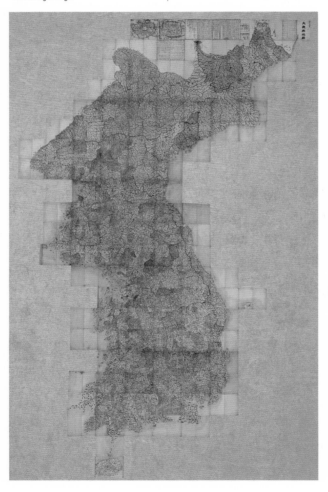

'Daedong yeojido'
We cannot view *Daedong yeojido* in its entirety today, partly because of its size. The map is as tall as a three-story building. This image shows a recent attractive colored rendering of it.
– Hwabong Mungo

Daedong yeojido in *Joseoneo dokbon* as part of their general effort to instill in the minds of young Koreans the notion that their country was inferior to Japan and therefore needed to follow the latter. In other words, it was part of colonial education aimed at raising little Koreans into

Provincial map of Tongyeong
The Daewongun ordered each county and prefecture in Joseon to produce a map of its territory and submit it to the central government. By 1872, 459 maps were completed. This photo shows the map of Tongyeong, in Gyeongsangnam-do Province, where the Sugun Tongjeyeong, the Joseon navy's headquarters, was located. It was from here that Admiral Yi Sunsin commanded the country's naval forces during the Japanese invasions.
– Kyujanggak Institute for Korean Studies

submissive individuals who would acquiesce unquestioningly to Japanese rule.

Japan would have wanted to emphasize the idea that Joseon was a backward country that couldn't even make a proper official map of its own, and that *Daedong yeojido* was the product of Kim Jeongho's efforts alone. It probably also sought to portray the Daewongun as an incompetent leader who was unable to appreciate the value of the map, and that its significance had instead been recognized by Japan.

After spreading widely during the colonial period, this version of Kim's story has persisted until today. It was even once included, word for word, in a fifth-grade elementary school Korean reading textbook in 1993. Fortunately, the version in today's equivalent textbook has been corrected, but several biographies still contain the fabrications I've just described. It's very frustrating.

Korean maps of the past

When did Korea first appear on a map of the world? Muslim cartographer Muhammad al-Idrisi's 1154 world map, *Tabula Rogeriana*, clearly shows the Korean Peninsula, which it labels "Sila." 1154 was well into the Goryeo period, but al-Idrisi appears to have thought that Silla still occupied the peninsula. What about early Korean cartographers? They produced everything from world to local maps, in a variety of designs and colors.

Interest in maps and geography reflects people's interests in the spaces they inhabit. Maps and geographical texts were also important sources of information for rulers as they governed their territories. Joseon's kings worked hard to produce the maps and texts they needed.

'Jeolla-do Mujanghyeondo' (Map of Mujang-hyeon in Jeolla-do)
This map gives a detailed view of government offices in Mujang-hyeon (today's Gochang-gun County), Jeolla-do Province. – National Museum of Korea

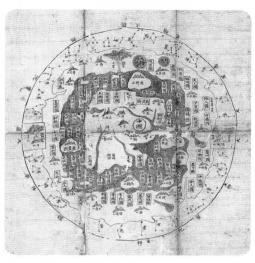

'Cheonhado' ('Map of the World') This round world map includes the constellations in the surrounding sky. – National Museum of Korea

'Cheonhado jido' ('Map of the World')
Produced in the 1790s, this world map was based on one found in the book *Zhifang waiji* ("Chronicle of Foreign Lands") by Giulio Aleni, an Italian missionary in Ming China. Features such as the North Pole, South Pole and equator are marked in Chinese. – Kyujanggak Institute for Korean Studies

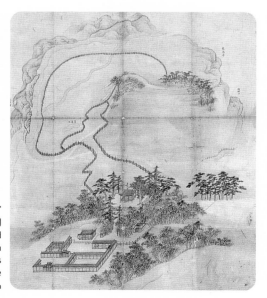

'Dongdaemun-oe Majangwon jeondo'
('Complete Map of the Majangwon Outside Dongdaemun Gate')
This map shows the Majang, a ranch where horses were raised, and the Majangwon, a government office that administered it. The ranch was located in what is now the Majang-dong neighborhood in Seoul's Seongdong-gu District. Today's Majang-dong is named after the Majang. – National Museum of Korea

CHAPTER 7

The peasants rise up

Farmers from several villages in the Jinju area began to gather. Soon, a meeting was in progress. On the agenda was the issue of what to do about the 160,000 *nyang* demanded in taxes, 100,000 by the local magistrate and 60,000 by provincial army commander Baek Naksin.

In fact, this was money destined to be embezzled by officials. It was natural that the innocent local peasants were furious about having to pay it.

TIME LINE --------- **1776** --------- **1780** -------- **1791** -------------

Joseon period
Jeongjo takes throne;
builds Gyujanggak

Park Jiwon travels to Qing;
writes *Yeolha ilgi*

'Keumnanjeongwon'
abolished except
for Yuguijeon

The Korean term minran, *used to denote a popular revolt, literally means "a disturbance among the people." This word is infused with the viewpoint of the ruling class: it implies that the people, who ought to be submissive, have disturbed the public order by coming together, rising up and making some sort of defiant demand.*

I prefer the Korean term nongmin bongi, *which can be translated as "peasant uprising." I think it expresses the stance of the peasants a little better.*

What do you think?

If the seventeenth and eighteenth centuries were an era of transformation, the nineteenth century was a time of peasant uprisings. This period saw a succession of huge revolts in various parts of the country.

What motivated the peasants to do this? These were the hardworking, simple farmers who had worked so hard to pick up the pieces in the devastating aftermath of the Japanese and Manchurian invasions. They had plowed over their ruined fields and developed new techniques like rice transplantation to increase production.

Today, let's look at the reasons for the peasant uprisings at this time. We'll need to go back to 1862 in the southeastern city of Jinju, where it all began.

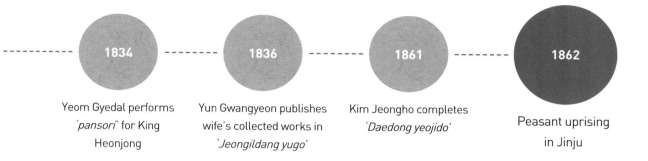

1834
Yeom Gyedal performs 'pansori' for King Heonjong

1836
Yun Gwangyeon publishes wife's collected works in 'Jeongildang yugo'

1861
Kim Jeongho completes 'Daedong yeojido'

1862
Peasant uprising in Jinju

It was January, 1862, in the village of Chukgok in Jinju, Gyeongsang-do Province. A lively discussion was taking place at the home of Geomdong, one of the villagers. In attendance were Yi Gyeyeol, a woodcutter, Yu Gyechun, a man of nominal *yangban* status who had fallen on hard times and was living as a farmer, former government official Yi Myeongyun, and several other villagers.

"The Jinju magistrate's demanding 100,000 *nyang* in tax, and Baek Naksin, the provincial army commander, wants 60,000. That's 160,000 nyang! We'll all starve trying to pay that much! What shall we do?"

"Good question. We need to come up with a plan."

"How about getting together and writing a petition?" said Yi, sounding distressed.

Jinju
This old map shows Jinju in Gyeongsangnam-do Province. In the Joseon period, Jinju was the biggest city in the province known as Gyeongsangu-do. Though today's Gyeongsang region is divided into two administrative provinces, Gyeongsangbuk-do ("North Gyeongsang") and Gyeongsangnam-do ("South Gyeongsang"), the Joseon period saw it divided into Gyeongsangjwa-do ("Left Gyeongsang") and Gyeongsangu-do ("Right Gyeongsang"), according to the point of view of the king in Hanyang as he sat facing south. It was in Jinju that the floodgates of the national peasant uprisings first opened.
–Kyujanggak Institute for Korean Studies

"A petition? Fat lot of good that would do," somebody else shouted back. "All we'd end up with is a beating. We have to think of something else."

The others nodded their heads and whispered among themselves.

"There's a market in Sugok village on the sixth of February," said Yu, the fallen *yangban*. "Let's start by gathering more people there."

"Good idea," chimed in Yi. "We can send out fliers so plenty of people turn up."

The south boils over

On the sixth of February, when the market in Sugok village opened as planned, farmers from several villages in the Jinju area began to gather. Soon, a meeting was in progress. On the agenda was the issue of what to do about the 160,000 *nyang* demanded in taxes, 100,000 by the local magistrate and 60,000 by provincial army commander Baek Naksin.

In fact, this was money destined to be embezzled by officials. It was natural that the innocent local peasants were furious about having to pay it.

The meeting revealed diverging opinions. While some called for a softer approach in the form of an official petition, other claimed that this was insufficient and that something more needed to be done. At this point, somebody cried out:

"Let's show them how strong we really are. We need to teach them a lesson for breaking our backs the whole time!"

A chorus of approval rang out.

"Let's put on white bandanas and dust off our clubs!" someone else shouted.

Finally, the peasants were off. They stormed towards Jinju town center, ransacking and burning the houses of several notorious officials on the way.

When provincial military commander Baek Naksin heard about the uprising, he made his way into town, confident that

Petitions
When commoners faced an intractable problem, they would sometimes seek official help by submitting a petition to a government office. A petition submitted by several people together was known as a *deungjang*, while one handed in by a single individual was called a *soji*. Government offices were obliged to provide appropriate replies to all petitions received.

Petty officials
Low-ranking officials working in provincial government offices were known as *ajeon* or *seori*. These included those in positions below the county governor, such as *ibang*, *hobang*, *yebang*, *byeongbang*, *hyeongbang* and *gongbang*. Among these ranks were many of the officials who squeezed the peasants hardest of all, making them the targets of particular wrath during the uprisings.

the peasants would back down once he had spoken to them. He had no idea how angry they were.

The farmers surrounded Baek and began remonstrating furiously with him about the way officials were pocketing taxes for themselves, then forcibly demanding even more tax, which they then siphoned off again... Baek was pinned down by a volley of accusations from all sides. Meanwhile, other farmers had caught clerk Gwon Junbeom and policeman Kim Huisun, two of the most notorious officials. After flogging them several dozen times, they threw the men into a fire. The clerk's son, Mandu, was also killed by angry peasants as he tried to save his father.

The peasants urged Baek to promise not to levy any more

Peasant uprising
The peasants of Jinju were incensed by the severe taxes demanded of them. Led by woodcutter Yi Gyeyeol and fallen *yangban* Yu Gyechun, they made their way to Jinju town center.

taxes. When the frightened official did so, they let him go. But this was not enough to assuage their anger. Now, they descended upon the homes of the vicious landowners who made their lives such a misery. Three of these were Jeong Namseong, Seong Buin and Choe Jinsa, tyrannical men who had incurred the deep resentment of the farmers obliged to rent their land. Soon, all of their houses were in flames.

Before long, word of the Jinju uprising reached neighboring villages. Here, too, the peasants faced hardships of a similar magnitude and were close to breaking point. Such villages were like tinderboxes, just waiting for somebody or something to provide a spark.

The peasant uprisings spread through Gyeongsang-do Province and into neighboring Jeolla-do and Chungcheong-do, sweeping through countless cities. All in all, a total of seventy-one uprisings occurred. But this was merely the official figure reported by the government; the actual number was much higher. Effectively, 1862 saw the entire southern part of the Korean Peninsula boil over.

Locations of uprisings

Kim Gyujin peasant uprising (1862)

Hong Gyeongnae uprising (1811)

Yu Gyechun Jinju peasant uprising (1862)

Peasant uprisings spread across the country like wildfire in the nineteenth century, when the country's farmers could no longer stand the sleaze and corruption that had been festering for years.

The excruciating tax burden

As you know, the Jinju uprising was prompted by taxes. Dissatisfaction with tax was far from confined to Jinju, however. The most unpopular taxes of all were *tojise*, *gunpo* and *hwangok*, known collectively as the *samjeong*. *Tojise* was a land tax; *gunpo* was a tax that all freeborn men between the age of sixteen and sixty had to pay; and *hwangok* was rice lent to farmers in the lean spring months that had to be repaid, with interest, after the harvest.

Normally, each kind of tax is paid by those eligible to pay it. *Tojise* was paid by those who owned land, while *hwangok* was paid by those who borrowed rice when they needed it and *gunpo* was only levied from those to whom it applied. At the time, however, tax was also paid by those who didn't need to, and even by those who couldn't afford it.

How did this happen? The fundamental cause lay in the national taxation system. The state would begin by deciding the total amount of tax to be paid by each region. After that, it was the responsibility of each region to come up with the money. If, for example, Jeolla-do had to pay a total of 100,000 *nyang*, it would be up to the villages in the region to collectively provide the required amount.

On top of this, the total amount of tax, once decided,

'Susepae'
These badges were worn by government tax collectors.
– National Museum of Korea

remained the same even if the amount of land to be taxed, or the number of men eligible to pay *gunpo*, decreased. As a result, each village was forced to resort to all kinds of unreasonable measures in order to meet its total tax bill.

Gunpo, for example, was levied even on newborn male babies, or on men who had died long ago. *Hwangok* revenues were increased by forcing high-interest rice loans even on people who didn't need them, or by lending sub-standard rice mixed with straw or sand. Yet another method was to rig scales when lending rice so as to give a smaller amount than that recorded, then claim back the full amount and resulting interest later on.

Peasants worked excruciatingly hard to meet these tax demands. *Aejeoryang* ("Lament for Severed Genitals") a poem by Silhak scholar Jeong Yagyong, conveys this hardship well. Living in exile in Gangjin, Jeong was able to

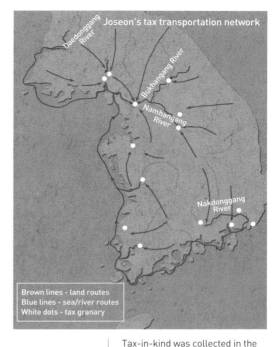

Joseon's tax transportation network

Daedonggang River
Bukhangang River
Namhangang River
Nakdonggang River

Brown lines - land routes
Blue lines - sea/river routes
White dots - tax granary

Tax-in-kind was collected in the provinces and sent to Seoul by boat. Official granaries were used to store grain collected as tax.

Joseon cargo boat (reproduction)
Cargo vessels like this one were used to transport tax-in-kind, collected in the provinces, all the way to the Hangang River.
– National Folk Museum of Korea

witness first-hand the suffering of the peasants around him.

My father-in-law is dead, and I stand in mourning clothes,
My baby boy is still wet behind the ears.
Yet still all three generations of our family
are on the *gunpo* register.

I could run to the government office and appeal,
But the door is guarded by a tiger of a man
and the local official will get angry and confiscate our only cow.

These are the words of a farmer's wife, lamenting how her late father-in-law and newborn son still have to pay *gunpo*.

But that wasn't all: tax collectors often creamed off money to line their own pockets, too. This was what led to the humiliation of Baek Naksin, the military official who triggered the Jinju uprising with his attempt to levy 60,000 *nyang* from local commoners and embezzle it for himself. To make matters worse, some influential people would bribe officials to avoid paying taxes.

No matter how much corruption went on, the government was satisfied as long as each village met its predetermined tax quota. As a result, peasants who submitted appeals at government offices were wasting their time. This was why the leaders of the Jinju uprising claimed that filing a petition would be useless and that the peasants had to give a show of force through solidarity.

Corruption and sleaze begin with dirty politics

The roots of corruption among local officials lay in the

How much tax did peasants pay?

In his book *Mongminsim seo*, Jeong Yagyong kept detailed records of the taxes farmers had to pay. According to the Silhak scholar, farmers in Jeolla-do normally harvested 600 *du* (a Joseon unit of capacity) of rice in an average year, 800 when there was a bumper harvest and 400 when there was a poor crop. Tenant farmers had to pay half of their harvest as rent to their landlords, so that in a typical year they would pay 300 *du* in rent and use the remaining 300 to feed themselves and pay taxes.

Farmers had to pay *tojise*, *gunpo* and *hwangok* totaling 76 *du* of rice per *gyeol* (a unit of area equivalent to a standard rice field, used to

Harvesting rice Farmers worked hard but were still not comfortably off. This painting is by late Joseon painter Sim Sajeong.
− National Museum of Korea

calculate tax payments). Which means that tenant farmers would pay around 25% of their 300 *du* in tax and have to live off the rest. This was not enough to feed a family of five for a year. Being left hungry after paying rent and tax was simply a fact of life for tenant farmers at the time.

National Folk
Museum of Korea

National Museum of Korea

country's elite ruling circles. At this time, the monarch was effectively a figurehead and true political power was in the hands of influential families such as the Kim clan of Andong and the Jo clan of Pungyang. Remember how I said the dominance of certain families is known as power politics?

In the days of power politics, officials descended into decadence. If they had pull with a powerful family, they could get away with anything. Government positions were frequently bought and sold for cash; officials who had purchased their posts were bound to use every trick in the book to levy more taxes and win back on their investments. In the midst of all this, it was helpless commoners that ended up paying the biggest price.

Meanwhile, *ajeon* and *yangban* would connive with other local officials to apply pressure directly to the farmers in their own villages. When an uprising broke out, these front-line tax collectors and greedy rich men became the primary targets of angry peasants. Their houses were pulled down and burned, while the tax registers were retrieved from government offices and flung onto the fire. This was why the peasants of Jinju killed Gwon Junbeom and other *ajeon* and burned down the houses of landowners. When peasant uprisings began spreading like wildfire, the government sent investigators to find out what was going on.

The state now gained a vague awareness that the unrest was caused by the chaos that reigned under the *samjeong* tax system. Park Gyusu, an envoy sent to Jinju, proposed to the king that a special government department be established to rectify the problems with the *samjeong*. His suggestion resulted in the creation of a new office called the Samjeong Correction Administration, although this new body eventually fizzled out without managing to fulfill its purpose.

Most peasants in late Joseon were tenant farmers with no land of their own. Most landowners, meanwhile, were *yangban*. The system at that time worked in such a way that tenant farmers had to pay high rents and taxes, whereas *yangban* owners weren't charged a penny. On top of this, the ruling class engaged in all kinds of corruption in order to increase its own wealth and honor. The peasant uprisings were a form of powerful criticism and resistance to this system and social order. And 1862 was the year when this discontent finally erupted like an angry volcano.

'Samjeong ijeong jeolmok'
This document produced by the Samjeong Correction Administration outlined the aspects of the tax system that needed fixing. The administration was set up by the government in response to the peasant uprisings in order to determine how to repair the *samjeong* system. It disappeared before it was able to take any proper action, however.

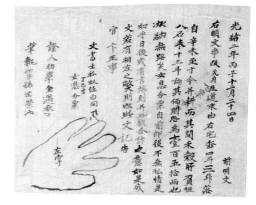

'Jamae mungi'
Documents in which individuals sold themselves or their family members into slavery were called *jamae mungi*. This one records how a man called Im Baekdong is selling his daugher, Bunsok, to his landlord to make up for five years' overdue rent.
−Chonbuk National University Museum

Hong Gyeongnae and the battle of Jeongju Fortress

Some fifty years before the Jinju peasant uprising, a huge rebellion took place in Pyeongan-do Province. This incident is known today as the Hong Gyeongnae uprising, after the man who led it.

Hong prepared for ten whole years before launching his rebellion. He opened a goldmine on Chotdaebong Peak in Unsan, gathered men, gave them military training, made counterfeit money on an island called Chudo, and used it to buy weapons. Finally, on December 18, 1811, Hong's rebellion began. At first, the rebel army was clearly the dominant side. In just ten days, it won control of the key areas of Pyeongan-do. As time passed, however, it began losing ground to government forces. The retreating rebels took refuge in Jeongjuseong Fortress. Local peasants joined them in order to avoid the wrath of the government troops, who were indiscriminately slaughtering innocent people at the time.

The government army surrounded the fortress and laid siege to it. Still, the people inside stood firm. Coming together as one, they offered solid resistance. As a last resort, the government forces dug a tunnel under the fortress wall, filled it with gunpowder early one morning and lit a fuse. The huge explosion that resulted caused the wall to collapse. Government troops now poured in and took the fortress. Hong's rebellion, which had lasted some 100 days, was over.

Hong Gyeongnae's uprising did not call for reform for the sake of peasants. But the four-month rebellion was enough to give the Joseon ruling class a proper fright. And it instilled peasants with the confidence to stand up to and fight against those who governed them. This proved a huge source of strength fifty years later, during the peasant uprisings that began in Jinju and swept through southern Joseon.

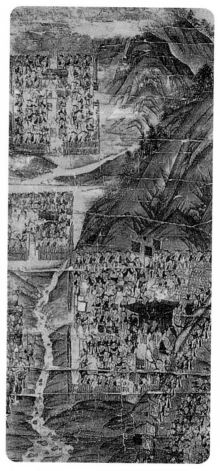

Government forces attack Jeongjuseong
Some 3,000 people were trapped in Jeongjuseong Fortress. Children below the age of ten and women were spared, while the remaining 1,900 were all put to death.

CHAPTER 8

Seohak and Donghak

The Western culture and religion entering Joseon this way was collectively labeled Seohak, meaning "Western learning." At first, it was the preserve of scholars, drawing such interest that every scholar or official worthy of the title had read at least one Seohak book. In most cases, however, this trend went no further than curiosity about Western science, technology and culture: Catholicism did not become the object of religious belief. Little by little, though, believers began to appear. Yi Seunghun was among them.

TIME
LINE

1864

1871

1876

Joseon period
Donghak leader Choe
Jeu executed

U.S. invasion
of Ganghwa-do

Treaty of Ganghwa signed
with Japan

The most striking of all the changes that occurred in late Joseon was the emergence of new ideas and religions. Specifically, Christianity arrived from the West. The religion is broadly divided into Catholicism and Protestantism; it was the former that first reached Joseon, followed later on by the latter.

Meanwhile, a new indigenous religion came into being amid criticism of Catholicism's radical nature and a search for ways to counter it. It was called Donghak.

How did Joseon's rulers cope with these changes? At the time, their worldview was dictated by Neo-Confucianism. Believing theirs to be the only correct system of thought, they looked down upon anything else as the activity of barbarians. The Joseon authorities banned all ideologies and religions except Neo-Confucianism, branding them sahak, *meaning "deviant learning."*

Despite the Joseon ruling class's refusal to recognize anything other than Neo-Confucianism, it was unable to stop the rapid spread of new ideas and religion throughout the country.

Today, let's take a look at what these were.

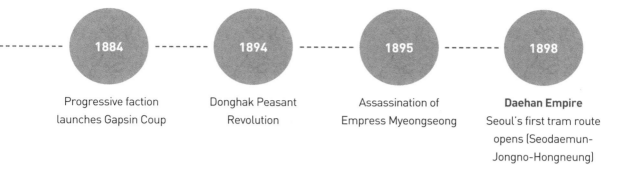

1884
Progressive faction launches Gapsin Coup

1894
Donghak Peasant Revolution

1895
Assassination of Empress Myeongseong

Daehan Empire
1898
Seoul's first tram route opens (Seodaemun-Jongno-Hongneung)

The first indication of Catholicism's existence reached Korea during the Japanese invasions. Konishi Yukinaga, one of the Japanese generals leading the invasion, was a devout Catholic. So were most of his subordinates. This was because Western Catholic missionaries, taking the lead in Asia, had reached Japan following their arrival in India and China and were working actively there. Konishi took a Portuguese priest named Gregorio Céspedes to Joseon for the sake of his Catholic men. Céspedes was the first Catholic priest to set foot there. He stayed with Konishi's men for about a year from late 1593, then went back to Japan.

Joseon's second encounter with Catholicism came after the Japanese invasion, when Yi Sugwang, an envoy to Ming, brought back a copy of Italian Jesuit priest Matteo

Matteo Ricci
Ricci, an Italian Jesuit priest, played a hugely important role in spreading Catholicism to Ming China. His book, *Tianzhu shiyi* ("The True Meaning of the Lord of Heaven"), was brought to Korea and translated into Hangeul.

Ricci's *Tianzhu shiyi*, which Ricci had written in Chinese to teach the people of Ming about the Catholic faith.

A third meeting occurred, as I mentioned to you some time ago in Volume III, during the Manchu invasions of Joseon, when Crown Prince Sohyeon was taken to Qing as a hostage. In Beijing, Sohyeon met German Jesuit Johann Adam Schall von Bell, who introduced him to Catholicism and various aspects of Western science and culture.

Neither Céspedes nor Sohyeon made much impact when it came to spreading Catholicism in Joseon. Even *Tianzhu shiyi*, brought back by Yi Sugwang, did not play much of a role in propagating the faith, despite being read by a few curious people.

Yi Seunghun: The first baptized Korean

The baptism of Yi Seunghun
Yi, among the members of a diplomatic mission to China, was baptized in Beijing by a Western priest.

In 1784, more than a century after the death of Crown Prince Sohyeon, a young Joseon man was baptized in the Qing capital, Beijing. His baptismal name was Peter, meaning "the rock," and he was the first Korean to undergo this Christian rite.

Western priests in Beijing were

amazed and quite moved to hear that a young man from the unknown land of Joseon had come to them and become a Catholic of his own accord. One of them expressed his feelings in a letter:

"He comes from Joseon, a peninsula to the east of China where no missionary has ever been. A diplomatic mission that arrived from there late last year visited our church. He was among its members: an exceptionally learned and cheerful young man, twenty-seven years old. Before he left again for Joseon, Father Grammont baptized him, giving him the name Peter."

Yi Seunghun was the brother-in-law of Silhak scholar Jeong Yagyong. He was born into a *yangban* family but interested in Catholicism and Western science and technology. When his father was sent as an envoy to Qing, Yi went with him to Beijing, where he met Catholic priests from the West.

Site of Cheonjinam
Cheonjinam was originally a Buddhist temple. Several figures interested in Catholicism, such as Yi Byeok, Gwon Cheolsin and Jeong Yakjong, gathered here to study and discuss Christian doctrine. Located in Gwangju, Gyeonggi-do Province, it is now a Catholic cemetery that contains the graves of Yi Byeok, Yi Seunghun, Jeong Yakjong and others.

Statue of Father Kim Daegeon
Kim was Korea's first Catholic priest. As a young man, he traveled with a Western priest to Macau, where he studied Theology and was ordained. Returning to Joseon, he began spreading the Catholic faith until he was arrested and put to death at the age of twenty-six. This photo shows the bronze statue of Father Kim that stands in front of Jeoldusan Martyrs' Museum in Hapjeong-dong, Mapo-gu, Seoul.

Around this time, quite a number of Koreans shared Yi's curiosity about Catholicism and Western culture. They took great interest in the books about the West brought back from Qing by returning envoys. The Western culture and religion entering Joseon this way was collectively labeled Seohak, meaning "Western learning." At first, it was the preserve of scholars, drawing such interest that every scholar or official worthy of the title had read at least one Seohak book. In most cases, however, this trend went no further than curiosity about Western science, technology and culture: Catholicism did not become the object of religious belief. Little by little, though, believers began to appear. Yi Seunghun was among them.

After his baptism, Yi returned to Joseon with items including catechisms, crucifixes, icons and rosaries and began spreading his faith to those around him. Every Sunday, he would meet with Yi Byeok, Jeong Yagyong and his brothers, Gwon Cheolsin and Kim Beomu at Kim's house in Myeongnyebang (today's Myeong-dong) in Seoul, where

Myeong-dong Cathedral
The most important Catholic place of worship in Korea, this cathedral stands in Seoul's Myeong-dong neighborhood. It was built on the site of the home of Kim Beomu, Korea's first Catholic martyr. This photo was taken in 1920.

they would hold mass and study doctrine. Kim's house thus became Korea's first Catholic church. This small group of men had established it by themselves, without being proselytized by foreign missionaries and without a priest appointed by the Pope.

One Sunday, soldiers sent by the State Tribunal burst into Kim's house and arrested the worshippers on charges of believing in a banned religion. As I mentioned earlier, every religion, thought system and academic discipline outside Neo-Confucianism was forbidden in Joseon at the time.

Most of the detained Catholics were released thanks to their *yangban* statuses, but Kim, a professional translator of *jungin* status, was sent into exile in Danyang, Chungcheong-do Province, where he died. This made Kim the first Korean Catholic martyr. The building we know today as Myeong-dong Cathedral appeared later on the site where Kim's house once stood.

왕이러러트시코오샤듸오회라죵용에코오디하놀이 유죵와대쇼민인등쳑샤륜음

명흥심을일온셩품이라ᄒ 명흥이러쳑오시민슌ᄒᄒ며야ᄒ덧덧흔셩품이

데ᄒ하민의게츙을나리오시 ᄒᄒ혀야ᄒ덧덧흔셩품이

이잇다ᄒ니 그ᄒ혼원비부

미콜온뎐이라ᄒ며근비부 말쥬란효쳐음을의논ᄒ면

ᄲ말ᄒ미요샹뎨노쥬지 말쥬란로쳐음을의논ᄒ 터로

온명이라ᄒ고홀온강튱이라ᄒ은슌단톄시쳠가릿 말쥬ᄒ며은슌톄시쳠가릿

치고고미잇솜이아니라 일리의운튱노바에두거

운이알션ᄒ며스셔말ᄉ 라란의운튱노바에일만이

물이셩육ᄒ여사룸이어더셩품됻재그덕이네히이

시니콜온인과의와례와지요그룬과다솟시이시니

'Cheoksa yuneum' ('Royal Decree on the Rejection of Deviant Beliefs')
This royal decree states that Joseon "rejects Catholicism, a wicked foreign belief." It was issued in 1839, during the reign of King Heonjong. The fact that the decree is written in Hangeul for easy comprehension by commoners shows that Catholicism was already widespread among the general public by this time.
– National Museum of Korea

Why Seohak was banned

The Joseon government outlawed Seohak on the grounds that it would disturb the social order upon which Neo-Confucianism was based, harm the country's ethics and morals, and challenge the authority of the state itself. At the time, Korean Catholics refused to hold ancestral rites, a stance that was regarded as an act of treason and a wholesale rejection of filial piety and loyalty, the most important Neo-Confucian virtues of all.

In 1791, a *yangban* and Seohak believer in Jinsan, Jeolla-do named Yun Jichung refused to conduct ancestral rites after his mother died. The government had Yun arrested and put to death for disturbing the social order and setting commoners a bad example. It then had all Seohak texts stored in royal palaces burned and decreed that anybody believing in the Western ideas or even found in possession of books about them from then on would be severely punished.

But Catholicism kept on spreading in secret. You will recall how many of Joseon's first Seohak believers were members of the Namin faction, which had lost out in a power struggle. Yi Seunghun, the first baptized Korean, was also a Namin. Because Seohak had spread among members of this defeated faction, it was often used as a pretext to persecute them, when in fact they were being harassed for political rather than religious reasons.

Persecution of Seohak believers began in earnest after the death of King Jeongjo. Many of the late monarch's most trusted ministers had been positively disposed towards Seohak. Now that he was gone, however, the newly ascendant Noron faction was able to have many of his closest advisors banished or executed for the crime of believing in the foreign ideas. The resulting Catholic Persecution of 1801 saw some 300 Catholics put to death, including Chinese missionary Father Zhou Wenmo.

Despite the strict government ban on belief in Seohak, it continued its steady spread through Joseon. Catholics were finally granted religious freedom in 1886—102 years after Yi Seunghun was baptized—when Joseon signed a treaty of commerce with France.

Quite a few Korean Catholics served as pawns for the interests of Western powers while ostensibly seeking religious freedom. Examples include Hwang Sayeong, who attempted in vain to deliver a letter to the Bishop of Beijing requesting a foreign attack on the Joseon government, and those who served as agents of Western armies during military campaigns

Jeoldusan Martyrs' Museum
Jeoldusan is a cliff that rises on the northern bank of the Hangang River in western Seoul. Originally called Yongdubong or Jamdubong, it acquired its current name, which means "Mt. Decapitation," after large numbers of Catholics were martyred there. Jeoldusan Martyrs' Museum was built in their memory.

against Korea by France in 1866 and the United States in 1871.

Donghak confronts Seohak

Just as foreign Seohak was spreading through Joseon, a new, indigenous religion was born. Founded by a man named Choe Jeu, it was called Donghak, meaning "Eastern learning." So why did Choe create this new religion, and how did it get its name?

Choe was born into a *yangban* family in Gyeongju in 1824. A bright boy, he studied Neo-Confucianism from a young age. When he was sixteen, though, his father died and he abandoned his studies to travel all over Joseon, seeing how people lived. What he found was commoners in truly dire circumstances. While the commoners were poorer than poor, the ruling class focused on accumulating ever more power and money. In the mean time, Seohak continued its rapid spread.

Choe wandered the country for a long time, at one point becoming engrossed in archery and horse racing, then dabbling in trade, then turning his attention to medicine and fortune-telling, then studying Buddhism and Seohak in search of ways of saving the world from chaos. Some fifteen years lates, he finally achieved enlightenment. *Donggyeong*

'Donggyeong daejeon' and 'Yongdam yusa'
Written by Choe Jeu, *Donggyeong daejeon* ("Bible of Donghak Doctrine") and *Yongdam yusa* ("Hymns from Dragon Pool") are the holy books of Donghak. They were burned at the time of Choe Jeu's execution, but later rewritten by Choe Sihyeong, the religion's second leader, who had memorized their entire content.

daejeon, the Donghak holy book, describes the scene when he received divine revelation from the Supreme Being.

One spring day in 1860, Choe was absorbed in prayer. Suddenly, he was overwhelmed by a strong feeling that left him light-headed and trembling. It was then that he heard a mysterious voice:

"Do not be afraid. The people of the world call me the Supreme Being. Why do you not recognize me?"

Choe was astonished.

"Why have you appeared before me, oh Supreme Being?" he asked.

"To send you forth into the world, that you may spread my law among the people. Do not doubt what I say."

"So you want me to teach people the way of Catholicism?"

"No. I have a divine talisman. It is called a *seonyak* and shaped like a *taegeuk* [the unified *yin* and *yang* symbol found at the

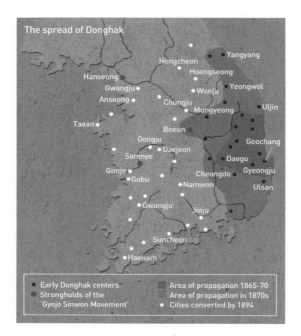

Yangyang
Hongcheon
Hoengseong
Hanseong
Gwangju
Wonju
Yeongwol
Anseong
Chungju
Taean
Mungyeong
Uljin
Boeun
Gongju
Geochang
Samnye
Daejeon
Daegu
Gimje
Cheongdo
Gyeongju
Gobu
Namwon
Ulsan
Gwangju
Jinju
Suncheon
Haenam

- Early Donghak centers
- Strongholds of the 'Gyojo Sinwon Movement'
- Area of propagation 1865-70
- Area of propagation in 1870s
- Cities converted by 1894

After starting in Gyeongsang-do Province, Donghak spread to Jeolla-do, Chungcheong-do and Gyeonggi-do, then on to other places throughout the country.

center of today's South Korean flag, the Taegeukgi] or the Chinese characters "弓弓." Take it, and save those who are suffering from disease. I will also teach you a spell: pass it on to others and let them serve me. Live long and work for the benefit of the world."

From then on, Choe began spreading Donghak far and wide.

By 1863, three years after its founding, Donghak had some 3,000 believers and diocese-like *jeop* in each region, headed by ministers called *jeopju* who gathered and taught believers.

Choe believed that Seohak was backed by the immense power of the West, and that, if left unchecked, its spread in Joseon would eventually lead to Western domination of the country. He was also more aware than anyone of the acute need for change and reform for the sake of the people. His concern was that without reform all of Joseon's commoners would be lost to the West: this is why he created a new religion.

Choe thought that since Neo-Confucianism couldn't deliver the change and reform that the people wanted, and that Seohak, though perhaps capable of bringing change and reform, would place Joseon under Western control, the only way to both achieve reform and win the hearts and minds of the people was to found a new religion. He therefore named his new faith Donghak, meaning "Eastern learning," as a symbol of opposition to Seohak.

Donghak contains a fusion of Confucianism, Buddhism and Taoism, as well as shamanistic beliefs and popular folk beliefs of its time, such as those contained in the prophetic text *Jeong Gam rok* ("Record of Jeong Gam"). And although it was founded to counter Seohak, Donghak accepts quite a few of the latter's good parts.

Cheondogyo Central Temple
Donghak was granted religious freedom in 1907, much later than either Catholicism or Protestantism and only after changing its name to Cheondoism. Cheondogyo Central Temple is located in Jongno-gu, Seoul.

Choe's religion has two central tenets: firstly, that man and the Supreme Being are one; and secondly, that this world will end and a new one will begin. The belief that humans and the Supreme Being are one and the same also signifies that the latter resides in every person, and that all people are therefore equal. This was a shocking claim in Joseon, which still upheld rigid social class divisions.

At the time, the royal court banned Donghak, branding it another wicked religion that would lead the people astray. The ruling class felt deeply threatened by Donghak's slogans of equality and the dawn of a new, better world. In March, 1864, the government captured Choe Jeu and had him executed in what is now Dalseong Park in Daegu.

Immediately before Choe Jeu was caught, he chose Choe Sihyeong to succeed him as leader of Donghak. While the former was of *yangban* origins, the latter was the son of a farmer. After being orphaned as a young boy, Choe Sihyeong had worked his way through various tough

Choe Sihyeong
Donghak's second leader, Choe contributed significantly to the spread of the faith. But he, too, was arrested and executed on charges of spreading a wicked religion.

'Jeong Gam rok'

This prophetic text, the title of which means "Record of Jeong Gam," was popular in the late Joseon period. It consists of conversations between two characters, Jeong Gam and Yi Sim, as they travel through scenic Mt. Geumgangsan.

The basic plot of the book is that the Yi Dynasty has had its day and that a "true man" by the name of Jeong will appear, found the Jeong Dynasty, and bring about a new world. Joseon will fall after 500 years, after which the Jeong Dynasty will rule from a capital at Mt. Gyeryongsan for 800 years. The fall of Joseon will be accompanied by a variety of omens and disasters; at this time, it will be safe to take refuge in a place called "Sipseungji." Its message about the fall of Joseon and the appearance of a new dynasty made *Jeong Gam rok* a work of treason as far as the ruling class was concerned. Copies were burned, and anybody discussing the book's content was severely punished. Still, its message continued to spread thanks to the popular longing for a better world.

jobs. He wandered all over the country, mixing with the people and spreading the message of Donghak. Some of his teachings were as follows:

"Donghak will come from within the kind of people who work in the fields and the woods."

"It's hard for the rich, the powerful and the well-educated to understand the Way."

"Hitting children is akin to hitting the Supreme Being. Don't do it."

Despite the government ban on Donghak, Choe Sihyeong's efforts increased the number of believers. Thirty years after Donghak had first spread among the peasants, in 1894, it acquired enough force to drive an uprising that rocked the entire Korean Peninsula. Donghak changed its name to Cheondoism in 1905 and still survives as a religion today.

Protestantism gains royal backing

Protestantism reached Korea around 100 years after Catholicism. The date of its arrival is generally considered to be September 22, 1884, the day Horace Allen, a medical missionary employed by the American embassy, first set foot in the country. At the time, Catholicism and Donghak were still banned. Yet Protestantism managed to win the favor of the king and began spreading rapidly with royal support. How did this happen?

Horace Allen and his wife
Ten years after arriving in Korea, Allen was appointed consul-general at the United States legation. This photo shows him and his wife in front of the legation; Allen is the tall man on the right.

Barely three months after Allen arrived, a reformist faction launched what we know today as the Gapsin Coup. This act presented the newly arrived missionary with a good opportunity: on the day it began, Min Yeongik, head of the conservative faction and a relative of the queen consort, was struck down by a swordsman at a party to celebrate the inauguration of the Postal Administration. Allen nursed Min back to health from his serious injuries, winning the deep gratitude of the king and queen. He became the royal couple's most trusted foreigner.

Thanks to Allen, other American missionaries also enjoyed the confidence of the Joseon authorities and were able to evangelize freely. The United States also won various special privileges, such as concessions for the gold mines at Mt. Unsan, the right to build a railway between Seoul and Incheon, and the right to build a tram network and waterworks in the capital. In April, 1885, seven months after Allen's arrival, Presbyterian missionary Horace Underwood and Methodist missionary Henry

Gwanghyewon
Built at the suggestion of Horace Allen, Gwanghyewon was Korea's first Western-style hospital. It went on to evolve into what is now Severance Hospital, located on the campus of Yonsei University in Seoul's Seodaemun-gu.

Appenzeller and his wife disembarked at Incheon. They were followed in turn, one month later, by William Scranton, another Methodist missionary, and his mother. From then on, the stream of missionaries kept flowing into Korea, bringing British Anglicans, Australian and Canadian Presbyterians, Baptists, Seventh-Day Adventists, the Salvation Army and so on. With the support of the royal court, they opened churches and schools and worked to spread the Protestant faith.

Quite a few Koreans took a positive view of Protestantism and adopted it as their own religion, believing it to offer a way of saving the country and improving the lives of the people. Famous examples include An Changho and Yi Sangjae. But with the signing of the Japan–Korea Protectorate Treaty of 1905 and Japan's growing domination of Korea, Protestantism gradually began leaning towards submission to Japan.

CHAPTER 9

Isolation or enlightenment? Korea at the crossroads

Over the years, though, the interests of the Western powers moved beyond trade. Now, they wanted to make the countries of East Asia into their own colonies. They scrambled to gain control of as much land in the region as possible, sending threatening gunships and forcing commercial treaties on any country that refused to trade with them voluntarily.

TIME LINE |-------- 1864 -------- 1871 -------- 1876 --------

Joseon period
Donghak leader Choe Jeu
executed

U.S. invasion
of Ganghwa-do

Treaty of Ganghwa signed
with Japan

We've now reached a very important point in Korean history: the moment when Western powers appeared and began dominating East Asia.

This time was of great significance for us today, as the head-on collision with the West that occurred here brought huge change.

The Western powers had been drawn to East Asia for several centuries already, lured by the promise of the spice trade. Some spices that grew only in Asia could be sold for a handsome profit back in Europe. Even Columbus's legendary discovery of the Americas came by accident as he sought an alternative route to India for transporting spices.

Over the years, though, the interests of the Western powers moved beyond trade. Now, they wanted to make the countries of East Asia into their own colonies. They scrambled to gain control of as much land in the region as possible, sending threatening gunships and forcing commercial treaties on any country that refused to trade with them voluntarily.

This kind of behavior is known as imperialism; it proved to be a successful way of conquering much of Africa, India and China.

Finally, the gunboats reached Joseon. So how did it respond?

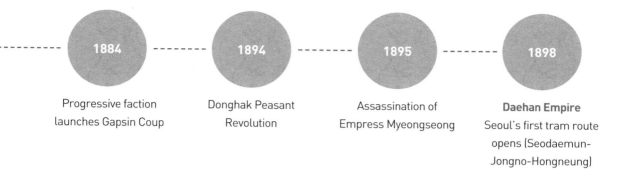

1884 ----- **1894** ----- **1895** ----- **1898**

Progressive faction
launches Gapsin Coup

Donghak Peasant
Revolution

Assassination of
Empress Myeongseong

Daehan Empire
Seoul's first tram route
opens (Seodaemun-
Jongno-Hongneung)

The first Western warship to appear off the coast of Korea was the Boussole, a French vessel under the command of Commodore Jean-François de Galaup, comte de Lapérouse. After reaching Jeju Island in May, 1787 and surveying its coastline, Lapérouse sailed on up the east coast of Korea until he reached another island. Claiming that he was the first to discover this piece of land and must therefore name it, he called his discovery Dagelet Island after Joseph Lepaute Dagelet, an astronomer accompanying him on the voyage.

Where on earth is Dagelet Island? It's the place we know today as

'Boussole'
This print shows the Boussole, under the command of Lapérouse, and her sistership the Astrolabe. Western ships began making frequent appearances off the coast of Joseon from the mid-eighteenth century onwards.

Ulleungdo. Lapérouse believed he had discovered it for the first time but, as you may know, Koreans had been familiar with it for centuries before that.

Other Westerners, just like Lapérouse, frequently named the unfamiliar lands they reached, believing they had discovered them for the first time. We can only conclude that they had little or no regard for the people who had already lived there for generations.

After the Boussole had gone on her way, other Western ships, from countries such as Britain, France, the United States and Russia, began arriving more often. Not knowing where they came from, the Joseon royal court simply called the vessels *iyangseon*, which literally means "different-looking ships."

The French navy attacks

Around the time more and more *iyangseon* were appearing in Korean waters, a truly shocking piece of news arrived: Qing had signed commercial treaties with the West and, still more amazingly, Britain and France had occupied the Qing capital, Beijing. Rumors spread that the so-called Western barbarians would soon be invading Joseon.

Joseon was then ruled by Yi Haeung, a man better known by his official title, Heungseon Daewongun. As father of young King Gojong, the Daewongun held the reins of power until his son reached adulthood. Finding himself in charge of a decrepit, crumbling state, he attempted to revive it with a combination of domestic policies to reinforce royal authority and a foreign policy of seclusion and total rejection of exchange with the West. The Daewongun didn't choose this closed-door policy from the word go. In fact, he was originally in favor of a degree of engagement with the outside world. But a series of events then persuaded him to change his mind.

In July 1866, three years after the Daewongun had taken power, the American merchant ship General Sherman sailed up the Daedonggang River to a point near Pyeongyang and demanded the right to trade with Joseon. Among the locals, however, a rumor went around that the true intention of the foreigners was to raid royal tombs in Pyeongyang.

Park Gyusu, the governor of Pyeongan-do Province, sent one of his men, Yi Hyeonik, to order the ship to leave. Instead, however, the General Sherman stayed where it was. Its crew claimed to be measuring the depth of the water. When Yi protested, the captain of the ship took him prisoner. At one point, the General Sherman even fired its cannons. Angered, the people of Pyeongyang filled several boats with gunpowder, ignited them and sent them floating toward the ship. It was soon on fire, and the crew who abandoned it were dragged out of the river and killed. This episode is now

Warning stone
The year after the French punitive expedition, the Daewongun had this stele erected at Deokjinjin. The message on it reads: "We have blocked the sea route into the country and are defending it. The ships of other states must not pass this point." This stone was put up four years before the so-called anti-foreigner steles.

Park Gyusu
Once a trusted official of the Daewongun, Park later changed his mind and began criticizing the closed-door policy and supporting the reformist movement. When the peasant uprising took place in Jinju, it was Park who traveled to the scene and reported back to the king that problems with the *samjeong* taxation system had to be solved. He was also the grandson of Silhak scholar Park Jiwon.

French forces on Ganghwa-do
This image shows French soldiers marching past Oegyujanggak, an annex of the Joseon royal library, during their 1866 campaign. It was painted by naval officer Jean Henri Zuber.

known as the General Sherman incident.

Two months later, a French fleet of seven warships carrying some 2,000 men attacked Ganghwa-do Island. Landing at Gapgot, they occupied the town of Ganghwa and struck camp. The French made several demands: compensation for the recent execution of nine French missionaries and other Korean Catholics, punishment of those responsible, and the signing of a treaty of commerce with Joseon.

Using incidents like the deaths of missionaries as a pretext for sending gunboats and demanding trade concessions was a favorite trick of Western imperial powers.

But Joseon didn't give in that easily. Its forces, under the command of Han Seonggeun and Yang Heonsu, put up fierce resistance at Munsusanseong and Jeongjoksanseong mountain fortresses. Judging the tide to have turned against his forces, French commander Rear Admiral Pierre-Gustave Roze ordered a withdrawal. The occupation had lasted one month.

The French forces stole plenty of valuable items as they withdrew, including cannons and arquebuses, other weapons, gold and silver, grain, and a large number of priceless books from Ganghwa-do Oegyujanggak, a local annex of the Joseon royal library. This incident is known in Korean as Byeongin Yangyo: *byeongin* was the calendar name of 1866 and *yangyo* means "disturbance caused by Westerners."

The Daewongun, his confidence boosted by victory against the French invaders, was now certain that a strict closed-door policy was better than opening Joseon to the barbarians through commercial treaties.

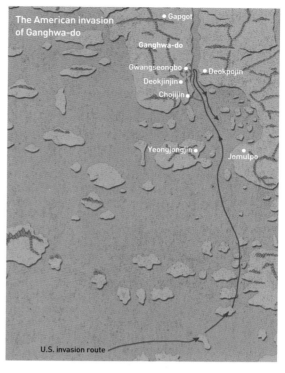

The American invasion of Ganghwa-do

- Gapgot
- Ganghwa-do
- Gwangseongbo
- Deokpojin
- Deokjinjin
- Chojijin
- Yeongjongjin
- Jemulpo

U.S. invasion route

The invading American forces sailed past Yeongjongdo Island, Chojijin and Deokjinjin to reach Gwangseongbo.

The American campaign and anti-foreigner steles

Five years after the French campaign against Joseon, the United States invaded. Citing the General Sherman incident

USS Colorado
This U.S. warship took part in the invasion of 1871.

Turret at Gwangseongbo
This turret, Yongdu Dondae, stands at the site of the decisive battle between Korean and American forces during the 1871 invasion. After two days of solid fighting, the Joseon side was becoming worn down by superior American firepower. Once all their bullets and arrows had run out, the Koreans fought on with their bare hands.

Cotton armor
Made from thirty layers of cotton, this armor was produced on the orders of the Daewongun and worn by Korean forces during the American invasion.

half a decade earlier, the American government sent a force of some 1,200 men on five warships to the waters off Ganghwa-do. Since the fiasco on the Daedonggang River, the U.S. had tried various ways of persuading Joseon to trade with it, even going as far as sending Qing-based German merchant Ernst Oppert on an unsuccessful mission to raid the tomb of Namyeongun, the Daewongun's father. The plan was to take Namyeongun's remains hostage, increasing the pressure on his son to reach a trade agreement with the Americans, but it ended in failure when Oppert was caught trying to open the tomb and had to make a hasty retreat. In fact, the incident backfired by enraging the Daewongun and further galvanizing his isolationist tendencies.

Faced with another American attack, the Daewongun again ordered the Joseon military to fight back. A fierce battle ensued at Gwangseongbo on Ganghwa-do. The Joseon

Sinmi Sunuichong
The remains of unidentified warriors who died in battle against the invading Americans in 1871 are buried in seven tombs at Gwangseongbo on Ganghwa-do.

forces fought bravely under the command of brothers Eo Jaeyeon and Jaesun.

But the American side boasted greatly superior firepower and the Joseon army inevitably found itself on the back foot. When it had no more bullets and arrows, its men resorted to hand-to-hand combat until they were virtually annihilated. To this day, their courageous sacrifice is commemorated by a stele that stands by their graves at Gwangseongbo. Following this victory, the American forces stopped fighting. After staying for about a month more, they withdrew. The incident is known in Korean as Sinmi Yangyo; *sinmi* is the calendar name of 1871 and *yangyo* means a "disturbance caused by foreigners."

The Daewongun, having now successfully blocked invasions by two of the world's great powers, drew the doors of his country even more tightly shut. He had steles erected at the main crossroads on Unjongga Street in Seoul and at other key places around the country, warning against making peace with barbarians. Known as *cheokhwabi* ("peace rejection steles"), they contained the following inscription:

"Failing to fight against barbarian invasions amounts to making peace. Calling for peace amounts to treason. This stele was made in the year *byeongin* [1866] and erected in the year *sinmi* [1871] as a warning to our descendants."

The Daewongun successfully united the will and strength of his people in resisting invasions by Western imperial powers. His repulsion of France and the United States was possible partly because of his unbending resolve, but

'Cheokhwabi' Steles such as this one were put up in key places around the country, instructiong the people of Joseon to resist Western invasions.

⚠ Missionaries, gunboats and comrnercial treaties

On board the Western warships during both the French and American invasions was a French Catholic missionary named Félix-Claire Ridel. Father Ridel had first entered Joseon in 1861, where he narrowly avoided execution for secretly spreading the Catholic faith and barely managed to escape the country again. His Korean name was Yi Bongmyeong. Now, he acted as a guide for the French and American forces, who had little knowledge of Korean geography.

The Western powers often used the deaths or injuries of missionaries as an excuse to turn up in heavily armed warships and demand trading privileges. When this happened, missionaries frequently served as guides for the invaders. Indian independence fighter and politician Jawaharlal Nehru once described such missionaries as "pawns of imperialism."

largely thanks to the strength and solidarity shown by his loyal and patriotic people.

The Daewongun's achievements

Heungseon Daewongun was Joseon's powerful regent for ten years, from 1863 to 1873. What he desired above all was to restore the supremacy of the Yi dynasty and the authority of the monarch, which had been eroded in the climate of power politics. He tried to achieve this through a combination of isolationist foreign policy and a variety of domestic reforms.

The Daewongun began by driving out the Andong Kim clan, a major player in the power politics of the time, and appointing a balanced cabinet of talented individuals. He abolished all but forty-seven of the country's private Confucian *seowon* academies, which had developed into hotbeds of political factionalism, and put an end to the traditional tax-exempt status of *yangban*. These reforms proved highly popular among his people.

Heungseon Daewongun Yi Haeung attempted to eradicate the power politics that had dominated Joseon for the previous sixty years and restore the authority of the throne. He held the position of regent, with the title Daewongun, for a ten-year period after his twelve-year-old son, Gojong, became king.

'Sangpyeongtongbo' (left) and 'dangbaekjeon' (right)
The Daewongun minted a new type of coin, called the *dangbaekjeon*, to cover the enormous cost of rebuilding Gyeongbokgung Palace. The *dangbaekjeon* was worth 100 of the *sangpyeongtongbo*, a coin used widely at the time. But the former was not suited to Joseon's economic reality; it caused soaring inflation and social instability. Ultimately, the government stopped producing the *dangbaekjeon* just six months after introducing it. –Bank of Korea Money Museum

The single-minded regent now set about rebuilding long-abandoned Gyeongbokgung Palace. This was the first palace built by Taejo Yi Seonggye after the founding of Joseon and had been the most important in the country. But after it was burned down during the Japanese invasions, Gyeongbokgung had remained abandoned for centuries as the royal court occupied other palaces such as Changdeokgung and Changgyeonggung. So why did the Daewongun choose to rebuild it now? This, too, was an attempt to restore the dignity that the king and royal family had enjoyed in the early years of Joseon.

Gun turret at Deokjinjin
As more and more Western ships started appearing off the coast of Joseon, the Daewongun reinforced the country's defenses in parts of Ganghwa-do. One example is this gun turret at Deokjinjin.

The ten years of the Daewongun's rule spanned a very important period in Korean history. The world was undergoing dramatic change, which eventually proved too much for Joseon's systems and society. The country needed to modernize.

Joseon had reached a critical juncture: a choice between developing independently, under its own strength; or experiencing forced modernization, unprepared, at the hands of foreign powers. The Daewongun had succeeded in uniting his people and blocking two foreign invasions, but he failed to use this same strength to bring about autonomous modernization. His aim was to revive the existing Joseon monarchy and its authority, not to build a new society altogether.

After the Daewongun stepped down, King Gojong began ruling the country directly. The young monarch took a different direction to that of his father, abandoning the policy of seclusion and opening Joseon's doors to the outside world. The challenge of independent modernization, however, remained unmet.

'Uigwe': Joseon texts seized by France

In Versailles, the French city famous for its magnificent palace, is an annex of the National Library of France. One day in 1979, Park Byeongseon, a Korean librarian at the annex, made a surprising discovery among a pile of books in the stacks, somewhere below the ground.

Park had stumbled across a *uigwe*, a type of Joseon royal protocol used to illustrate and describe the procedures involved in key state occasions. Such documents are an immensely valuable part of Korean cultural heritage today. How on earth had a Joseon-era *uigwe* made its way so far into the bowels of France's national library? It turned out that several hundred such protocols had been taken from Ganghwa-do by French troops during their short-lived invasion of Joseon in 1866. A letter from Rear Admiral Pierre-Gustave Roze, commander of the invasion, to one of his superiors contains the following passage:

Oegyujanggak
This annex of Gyujanggak, the royal library that stands in the grounds of Seoul's Changdeokgung Palace, was built inside the Ganghwahaenggung Temporary Palace complex to store valuable books. It was recently restored, long after being burned down by French forces during their 1866 invasion. Since 1990, Korea has been requesting the return of books snatched by the French from Oegyujanggak, but the issue remains unresolved. This photo shows a nineteenth-century map called *Ganghwa bugung jeondo* ("Map of the Palace at Ganghwa")

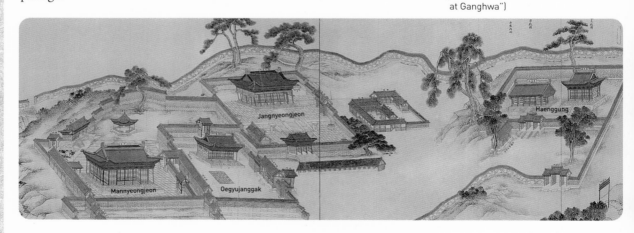

"At a house where the king of Joseon sometimes comes to stay is a reading room of extremely valuable-looking books. We have carefully packaged 340 of them and I will send them to France at the first available opportunity."

The "house" of which Roze wrote was Ganghwahaenggung Temporary Palace, and the "reading room" refers to

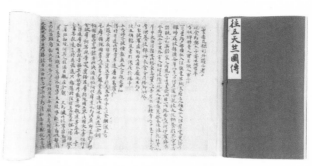

'Wang ocheonchukguk jeon' (copy)
– Independence Hall of Korea

Oegyujanggak, an annex of the Seoul-based royal library, Gyujanggak. The annex contained some 6,000 volumes at the time; the French forces took away 340 and burned the rest, along with the building that housed them.

In addition to several *uigwe*, the National Library of France houses other Korean texts such as *Cheonsang yeolcha bunyajido* ("Planisphere Chart of Different Celestial Zones"), a star map produced during the reign of King Taejo; a volume of *Jikji* (an abbreviation of the full Korean title of "Anthology of Great Buddhist Priests' Zen Teachings"), the world's oldest extant work printed using movable metal type; and a manuscript of *Wang ocheonchukguk jeon* ("Memoirs of a Pilgrimage to the Five Indian Kingdoms") by the Silla Buddhist monk Hyecho. Much of Korea's cultural heritage is scattered throughout not just France but many other countries, including Japan, the United States, Russia and Germany. Why? Western powers unfailingly took away many national treasures from the countries they invaded. A large proportion of the artworks and other items housed in institutions like the Louvre, the British Museum and the Vatican Museum were taken from other countries during the age of imperialism.

CHAPTER 10

Opening the doors

Which direction was right for Joseon at the time? What would you have decided on?

The signing of a treaty between two countries requires detailed preparation. You need to analyze the potential effects of the treaty on your own state, then negotiate with the other party to reach conditions that bring you the greatest possible advantage. But the Joseon royal court was seriously unprepared when it signed the Treaty of Ganghwa.

TIME
LINE

1864

1871

1876

Joseon period
Donghak leader Choe Jeu
executed

U.S. invasion of
Ganghwa-do

Treaty of Ganghwa
signed with Japan

Have you ever heard of the Treaty of Ganghwa?

It was the first treaty ever signed by Korea with Japan—or with any other country, for that matter.

The agreement is officially called "Byeongja suho jogyu," meaning "1876 Stipulation of Amity," but is commonly referred to as the Treaty of Ganghwa because that's where it was signed.

The Treaty of Ganghwa marked the end of Joseon's self-imposed isolation and opened the country's doors. It now found itself face to face not only with Japan but with other powers such as the United States, Britain, Russia and France.

Until now, Qing had been the most important foreign country in the minds of most Koreans, and the country's rulers had only paid serious attention to relations with their giant neighbor to the north. The Treaty of Ganghwa marked Joseon's first step onto the wider world stage.

It was hardly a hopeful step, however.

This was an age of empires, where powerful states attacked their weaker counterparts and made them into colonies. Any country that wanted to evade the tentacles of the great powers had to have its wits about it.

Unfortunately, Joseon did not.

Today, we'll be taking a look at the Treaty of Ganghwa.

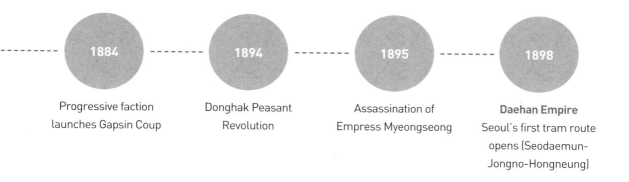

1884
Progressive faction launches Gapsin Coup

1894
Donghak Peasant Revolution

1895
Assassination of Empress Myeongseong

1898
Daehan Empire
Seoul's first tram route opens (Seodaemun-Jongno-Hongneung)

Military bases on Ganghwa-do
This map shows the positions of *jin*, *bo* and *dondae*, three types of military installation, on Ganghwa-do. They were built all along the coast of the island.
– National Palace Museum of Korea

One day in 1875, when Joseon still hadn't quite got over the shock of the recent French and American invasions, an unfamiliar ship appeared off the coast of Chojijin on Ganghwa-do. It dropped a smaller boat into the water, which began to approach the shore. Joseon military forces guarding the area fired their cannons at the unidentified and unannounced boat as it approached. Its crew returned fire, but soon turned back.

Now, though, the larger ship began firing its cannons at Chojijin. They were incomparably more powerful than the outdated Joseon guns. Some time later, the ship slunk off again. Where had it come from? And why had it appeared at Ganghwa-do?

'Unyo' This Japanese warship appeared off Chojijin on September 20, 1875 and began firing its cannons. The incident was deliberately engineered by Japan as part of a plan to conclude a commercial treaty with Joseon.

Chojijin Can you see the sea beyond the fortress wall here? Chojijin was the first Joseon military installation encountered by ships sailing past Ganghwa-do from the Yellow Sea. This was the site of both the Unyo incident and the American invasion four years earlier. You can still see the marks left by Japanese cannonballs on the fortress walls.

Japan's attack on Ganghwa and the 'Unyo' incident

The strange vessel that had approached Ganghwa was the Unyo, a Japanese warship with a military crew. Instead of heading straight home, the ship stopped at Yeongjongdo Island, where Incheon International Airport now stands, killed several innocent Koreans, and burned down their houses. Only then did it set sail for Japan.

The unprovoked attack left Joseon angry and confused. It was clear that Japan had to be held to account for its actions. On the contrary, however, Japan now began harshly criticizing

Joseon, having manufactured the entire incident as part of a plan to force the latter into a trading relationship.

Right on cue, Japan began remonstrating with Joseon: the Unyo had only approached Chojijin to look for some fresh water. When the Joseon army suddenly started attacking, it had had no choice but to defend itself. Japan then dispatched three warships to Busan, claiming that the lives of Japanese expatriates there may be in danger. The vessels lined up in front of the city and started firing their guns indiscriminately. The frightened people of Joseon had no idea what was going on.

Demanding that Joseon take responsibility for the Unyo incident, Japan sent two representatives, Kuroda Kiyotaka and Inoue Kaoru, to Busan.

"Japan will send a minister to Ganghwa-do for talks with his Korean counterpart," they announced. "If the Korean minister refuses to show up, we will immediately attack Hanyang."

The Joseon royal court hastily sent Sin Heon, head of the Security Council, to Ganghwa-do and discussed how to respond to its eastern neighbor. The court's view was that the Japanese military should be prevented from landing on Ganghwa-do at all costs. When Sin arrived at the island, however, he found Japanese ships waiting off the coast. In the end, he was unable to stop the troops and envoys landing

Sin Heon
Sin was Joseon's main representative in the negotiations that led to the signing of the Treaty of Ganghwa, and in later talks on a commerce treaty with the United States. He also supported Kim Jeongho during the production of *Daedong yeojido*.

Yeonmudang Hall, Ganghwa-do
It was here that the Ganghwa treaty talks took place. This photo dates from 1876.

Site of Yeonmudang today
The hall itself no longer stands, leaving a plot that contains only this memorial.

on Joseon soil.

Talks began the next day. The Japanese side was represented by Kuroda and Inoue, plus two more men named Miyamoto and Moriyama. Sin Heon, Yun Jaseung, Hong Daejung and Gang Wi negotiated on behalf of Joseon. Three rounds of talks were held, at which Japan laid out a copy of the treaty it had already drafted and threatened the Joseon side:

"If we don't receive an answer within ten days, the present state of good relations between Japan and Joseon will no longer apply."

The Joseon court now faced a dilemma. The "end of good relations" implicitly meant the possibility of war. The country's leaders mulled over the implications of both options: accepting Japan's demands and signing the treaty; and refusing. A letter now arrived from Qing:

Joseon and Japan delegates sign the Treaty of Ganghwa
From Joseon's perspective, the Treaty of Ganghwa was signed without the chance for much preparation. Its officials knew little about the laws and treaties governing international society at the time and ended up agreeing to an unequal treaty that worked unilaterally in the interests of Japan.

"If you sign a treaty with Japan, war will be avoided. If you ignore this advice, we will not be responsible for whatever happens next."

Qing had sent this message at Japan's request. Joseon, its hands tied, decided to sign the treaty with Japan. It wasn't well versed in international law at this point, however, and agreed to the Japanese-drafted version of the treaty with hardly any modifications of its own.

Finally, on February 3, 1876, the Joseon and Japanese representatives put their national seals to the treaty at a ceremony in Yeonmudang Hall on Ganghwa-do. This became what we now know as the Treaty of Ganghwa.

Japan's ambitions

Why did Japan want to sign a treaty with Joseon? This was a country that had once operated a closed-door policy just

The opening of Japan
Japan was forced by the United States to open its doors some twenty years before the Treaty of Ganghwa. After that, it began a rapid transformation. This print is of a scene from Yokohama, a treaty port, in 1859. On the hill to the right are the houses of foreigners.

like that of its neighbor—for much longer, in fact. Japan had previously kept its borders sealed for some 200 years.

Just like other East Asian states, stubbornly isolationist Japan had been forced to sign a treaty of commerce and open its doors when the wave of Western imperialism hit. In Japan's case, the source of coercion was the United States.

Japan and America had signed a "treaty of amity and commerce" after the arrival of Commodore Matthew Perry with warships and cannons in 1854, around twenty years before the Unyo incident. Japan went on to sign treaties with Britain, Russia, the Netherlands and France.

After opening its doors, the island nation began a rapid transformation. It sent inspection teams to several Western nations to learn about their laws, systems, industries and cultures, then began a swift process of modernization by applying to itself the knowledge that its inspectors had gathered. In the mean time, many Japanese went to study at foreign universities and learn more about Western academic disciplines.

Japan's ambition went beyond self-modernization: it wanted to join the ranks of the Western imperial states. The rising

Discussing the conquest of Korea
Many Japanese in the late-
nineteenth century argued that
their country should conquer
Korea.

power went all-out to acquire colonies like its Western role models. And the first country to fall in its sights was Joseon. The Treaty of Ganghwa was the initial step in Japan's plan to colonize the peninsula.

Japan now deployed the method that had been used on it by the United States twenty years ago: a semi-coerced treaty, signed with large gunboats looming in the background. The content of the actual text, meanwhile, was modeled on the 1858 Anglo-Japanese Treaty of Amity and Commerce. Despite this, Joseon remained unaware of the dramatic changes underfoot in Japan and continued to look down on its people as barbarians.

Another reason for Joseon's signing of the Treaty of Ganghwa was the huge political change the country had undergone. Heungseon Daewongun had stepped down and Gojong was now in charge. With the king now a twenty-two-year-old adult, his father's continued domination of politics on his behalf could no longer be justified. Gojong's wife, Queen

Min, had also urged him to persude the regent to stand down. You may well have heard of Queen Min, perhaps under her better-known later title, Empress Myeongseong.

Once the Daewongun had stepped down, Queen Min became a staunch supporter of Gojong. The king placed many of his wife's relatives in key government positions and the royal couple abandoned the former regent's closed-door policy, choosing a path of "enlightenment" instead. Joseon's signing of the Treaty of Ganghwa, then, happened because of the choices made by Gojong and Min. The situation may well have been different had the Daewongun still been in power.

An unprepared, unequal treaty

In the late-nineteenth century, Joseon had reached a fork in the road. It now had to make weighty choices between isolation and opening, and between tradition and "enlightenment." The choices of the Daewongun were different to those made by King Gojong and Queen Min. The former opted for closed doors, while the latter chose enlightenment. Which direction was right for Joseon at the time? What would you have decided on?

The signing of a treaty between two countries requires detailed preparation. You need to analyze the potential effects of the treaty on your own state, then negotiate with

The Treaty of Ganghwa contains twelve articles. These are the most important among them:
• **Article 1:** Joseon is an independent state and enjoys the same rights as Japan.
• **Articles 4 and 5:** The Joseon government will open Busan and two other ports, allowing free access and trading rights to Japanese citizens.
• **Article 7:** Japanese navigators are allowed to freely survey the Joseon coastline.
• **Article 9:** Citizens of Joseon and Japan are allowed to trade freely with each other; no interference whatsoever in such trade by officials from either state is permitted.
• **Article 10:** All cases related to crimes committed by Japanese citizens in treaty ports designated by Joseon and involving Joseon citizens will be tried by Japanese officials.

Jemulpo in the treaty port period
The Treaty of Ganghwa stipulated that Joseon would open three ports: Busan, Incheon and Wonsan. This photo shows the Jemulpo area of Incheon just after the port was opened.

the other party to reach conditions that bring you the greatest possible advantage. But the Joseon royal court was seriously unprepared when it signed the Treaty of Ganghwa. The king and queen had merely talked about enlightenment, rather than actually doing much to achieve it.

To make matters worse, Joseon didn't know much about the laws and treaties in force in international society at the time. The government ended up signing the treaty without realizing its significance or the effects it would have.

According to the Treaty of Ganghwa, Joseon would open the ports of Busan, Wonsan and Incheon, allowing Japanese the freedom to visit and conduct trade as they wished. Places where these freedoms are granted are known as treaty ports. The Treaty of Ganghwa worked unilaterally in Japan's favor and was disadvantageous for Joseon in several ways, as I'll now explain.

Article 1 of the treaty stated, "Joseon is an independent state and enjoys the same rights as Japan." This seems fair enough at first glance, but its secret purpose was in fact to place distance between Joseon and Qing. Describing Joseon as an independent state indicated that it had nothing to do with Qing. Since acknowledging that Joseon was under the influence of its Chinese neighbor would entail interference by the latter in its political affairs, this article was inserted to preempt such a possibility.

Article 10, too, worked entirely to Japan's advantage by granting extraterritoriality to its citizens in Joseon, putting them beyond the reach of the local justice system. Korea still grants extraterritoriality to American troops posted on its soil, which is a source of much controversy.

The hidden purpose of tariffs

The most serious issue with the Treaty of Ganghwa was that of tariffs, the taxes levied on imports and exports. Japan's suggestion was as follows:

"Japan has chosen not to levy taxes on any of the goods it exports to Joseon. Tax will therefore not be levied on goods imported into Japan from Joseon either."

Joseon accepted this, believing it could have nothing to lose if both sides abolished tariffs in just the same way. As a result, no charges were imposed on goods flowing in either direction between the two states.

But this arrangement hid a serious problem. On the surface, it may have appeared fair that neither country levied tariffs on the other's goods. But Japanese exports to Joseon were mass-produced items, whereas most of Joseon's exports to Japan consisted of rice and other agricultural produce. Scholar Yu Giljun penetrated the heart of the problem in his book *Seoyu gyeonmun* ("Observations on a Journey to the West"):

"The products Japan exports to Joseon are machine-made and can be produced in infinite numbers. But the agricultural products Joseon exports to Japan come from the land and are therefore finite. The more trade between the two countries grows, the greater Joseon's material loss will be."

Before long, Yu's observation proved to be correct.

Let's take a closer look at tariffs. They have two functions: increasing state revenue and protecting the national economy.

Take cars, for example. What happens if cars made in a

Yu Giljun and '*Seoyu gyeonmun*' After studying in the United States, Yu Giljun traveled the world on his way back to Korea. He visited several major European capitals. *Seoyu gyeonmun*, his account of this journey, is characterized by its mixed use of Chinese characters and Hangeul. Published in Japan in 1895, it is full of information about European laws, systems, culture and education. The photo above was taken while Yu was in Japan, after writing *Seoyu gyeonmun*. He sits in the front row, second from the left.
–Korea University Museum

country with much better technology than Korea are imported and sold at the same price as Korean cars, or cheaper? Korean cars will no longer sell, car factories will shut down and the Korean car industry will be snuffed out in its infancy without ever having had the chance to develop.

This is where the role of tariffs comes in: until one

Special envoy Kim Gisu tours Japan

Straight after signing the Treaty of Ganghwa, Joseon sent a fact-finding mission to Japan. When he arrived, delegation head Kim Gisu couldn't believe his eyes. Having previously known only Joseon and Qing, he was dazzled by Japan's well-developed industry and culture. He wrote about his feelings as follows:

"There are many cities across the country. The houses and shops I saw in the cities I visited myself, such as Tokyo, Yokohama and Kobe, appeared highly prosperous. Having never witnessed such magnificent scenes, I was naturally astonished. Even people like Yi Yongsuk, who has been to Qing several times, praised the country for its far higher levels of wealth and abundance than those of Qing."

The Joseon mission in Japan
Kim Gisu led a group of Joseon officials on a trip to Japan in 1876. They spent some twenty days there, observing Japanese culture, before returning to Joseon.

country's industries and technology are sufficiently developed to compete with foreign rivals, its government will impose high tariffs on imports to protect domestic industries and the economy as a whole. When it signed the Treaty of Ganghwa, however, the Joseon government was completely unaware of this important function of tariffs. If only it had been...

Well, that should give you some idea of why the Treaty of Ganghwa was unequal, working only in Japan's interests and against those of Joseon. Once it was signed, the latter could no longer view Qing as the only relevant foreign power. Japan was followed by a stream of Western states demanding commercal treaties of their own: Joseon ended up entering such agreements with the United States, Britain, Russia, Italy, France and Austria. It now found itself part of a much more complicated international order.

A 'Treaty of Peace, Amity, Commerce and Navigation'

The United States was the second foreign power to sign a treaty with Joseon. It did so in June, 1882, six years after Japan. America had continued seeking to trade with Joseon after its abortive invasion in 1871. When it heard that the kingdom had signed a treaty with Japan, it sent Commodore Robert Shufeldt to attempt negotiations.

At this time, a book titled *Joseon chaengnyak* ("Joseon Strategy") had caused quite a stir. Written by Huang Zunxian, a Qing official working in Japan, the book claimed that Joseon should "be wary of Russia and join forces with Qing, Japan and the United States."

Gojong took interest in the book, encouraging his ministers and Confucian scholars throughout the country to read it. Advocates of enlightenment welcomed the text, but Confucians strongly opposed it. Yi Manson, a descendant of Toegye Yi Hwang, gathered the names of 11,000 Confucian scholars in the southeastern Yeongnam region of Korea and submitted a petition opposing the book's content. This petition is known in Korean as "Yeongnam maninso," literally, "the 10,000-name petition of Yeongnam."

But Gojong had Yi Manson banished to a far-flung island and sent Kim Yunsik to Qing to discuss a potential treaty with America. Kim himself never met Shufeldt: instead, negotiations with the American were conducted by Qing representative Li Hongzhang, a strategy used by Qing to maintain its influence over Joseon.

The treaty was signed in 1882 in a specially-erected marquee in Jemulpo, Incheon. The single most salient aspect of the agreement, officially titled "A Treaty of Peace, Amity, Commerce and Navigation," was the way it granted the United States "most-favored-nation" status. This article meant that any privileges granted to other states later on by Joseon would automatically apply to the U.S. as well.

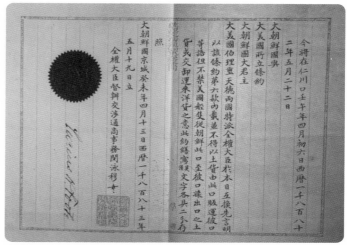

Treaty of peace, amity, commerce and navigation
This treaty between Joseon and the United States is written in courteous, dignified language. Behind this stylistic façade, however, is content that puts the US at a great advantage by according it most-favored-nation status.
–National Institute of Korean History

Any special rights Joseon now granted in other treaties to France or Britain, for example, would automatically extend to America, which could simply put its feet up as other countries won it more and more privileges. The most-favored-nation article brought the United States greater benefits than any other country in Korea.

CHAPTER 11

'A new world, for three days': the Gapsin Coup

At ten o'clock that night, just when the party had reached full swing, somebody shouted: "Fire!" Min Yeongik, whose status as a relative of Queen Min made him one of the most powerful men in the country, ran outside the building. Shortly afterwards, he staggered back inside, bleeding, and collapsed. He had been stabbed in an ambush by members of the progressive faction. The party descended into chaos as its guests began to flee. This was the first act of the Gapsin Coup.

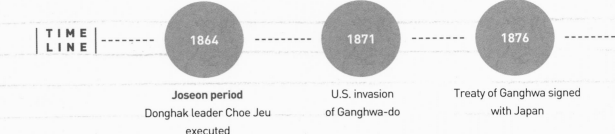

TIME LINE

1864

1871

1876

Joseon period
Donghak leader Choe Jeu
executed

U.S. invasion
of Ganghwa-do

Treaty of Ganghwa signed
with Japan

Today, I'd like to tell you about the so-called "Gapsin Coup," a movement launched by a group of young and highly spirited officials. The men involved belonged to what was known as the "enlightenment faction," a group who believed in the need to embrace advanced Western culture in order to modernize the state and society in Joseon.

So what were the aims of their coup?

Joseon faced a very complicated situation in the late-nineteenth century. After signing the Treaty of Ganghwa, it found itself under growing pressure from various Western powers and was forced to rapidly gather its wits.

The country now faced two major challenges: defending itself from the foreign powers that threatened to invade at any time, and reforming its society to achieve modernization.

Rising to these two tasks was the only way Joseon and its people could expect to avoid serious trouble. And there was a long queue of movements trying to do just that.

Today, I'd like to tell you about the Gapsin Coup and the enlightenment faction that launched it.

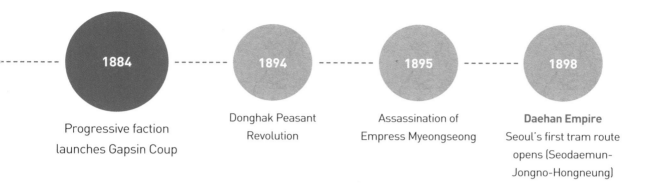

1884
Progressive faction launches Gapsin Coup

1894
Donghak Peasant Revolution

1895
Assassination of Empress Myeongseong

1898
Daehan Empire
Seoul's first tram route opens (Seodaemun-Jongno-Hongneung)

Members of the enlightenment faction—we might also call them "progressives"—believed that policies of openness and rapid change were the best way to develop the country. Leading Korean progressives at this time included Kim Okgyun, Park Yeonghyo, Seo Gwangbeom, Hong Yeongsik and Seo Jaepil. They called for rapid change modeled on that of Japan, and for the elimination of Queen Min and the rest of her faction, who were politically dependent upon Qing. Branded conservatives by the progressives, the Min faction claimed Qing was the only buffer that could protect Joseon, and

Former comrades
This commemorative photo shows the members of the Bobingsa, the first mission sent from Joseon to the United States. It was taken in 1883, one year before the Gapsin Coup. Sitting in the front row, from the second figure from the right, are Seo Gwangbeom, Min Yeongik and Hong Yeongsik. The third figure from the left in the back row is Yu Giljun. Before the coup, members of the progressive and conservative factions were comrades. That's why we see progressives Seo, Hong and Yu in the same photo as conservative Min.

advocated reform modeled on that of the giant empire.

The members of the progressive and conservative factions had once been comrades. All of them were bright young men from *yangban* families, who had been educated by figures such as Park Gyusu, O Gyeongseok and Yu Honggi.

A split into two factions

Park Gyusu, once a trusted official of the Daewongun, became a progressive. His mind was changed by a visit to Qing; he now believed Joseon must embrace the more advanced culture of the West and undergo reform, rather than sticking to a closed-door policy like that of the inward-looking regent. Park invited bright young *yangban* men to his study, where he introduced them to Western culture and strongly emphasized that sweeping reform was needed to save Joseon. His home became a hotbed of enlightenment thought.

O Gyeongseok and Yu Honggi, like Park, worked hard to spread progressive ideology. The two men were of the same age and shared *jungin* status: O was a translator and Yu a physician. They even lived close to each other, with Yu's house in Gwancheol-dong to the east of Cheonggyecheon Stream and O's in Samgak-dong to the west.

As a translator, O made frequent trips to Qing and was alert to the changes he saw on his travels. He brought back books on Western history, geography and science, such as *Yinghuan zhilue* ("A Short Account of the Maritime Circuit"), *Yi yan* ("On Change") and *Haiguo tuzhi* ("Illustrated Treatise on the Maritime Kingdoms"), which he studied together with Yu. Despite their *jungin* status, the two men managed to transcend the class barrier and sow dreams of progress in the minds of *yangban* boys like Kim Okgyun, Park Yeonghyo and Kim Yunsik.

After a while, however, the young enlightenment visionaries split into two factions: the progressives, who called for rapid reform modeled on that of Japan; and the conservatives, who advocated more gradual change based on that of Qing. You might say both factions agreed on the need for reform, but differed when it came to the ideal method and speed. The former friends now became enemies.

The progressive faction, led by Kim Okgyun, began preparing its revolution in spring, 1884. Japan knew about their

'Yinghuan zhilue'
Written in 1848 by Qing scholar official Xu Jiyu, this book brings together the histories, geographies, sciences and cultures of various countries. It was ideal for readers seeking to know more about the world, and a favorite book of O Gyeongseok and Yu Honggi.
– Jeju National Museum

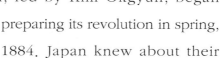
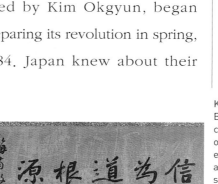

University of Seoul Museum

Independence Hall of Korea

Kim Okgyun and his calligraphy
Born into the illustrious Andong Kim clan, Okgyun was a promising young official who had passed the state examination with the highest score among all sitting candidates. His social, writing and speaking skills are said to have been outstanding. On the left is a portrait of Kim, next to a sample of his handwriting that reads "trust is the basis of the Way."

plan and had promised to help, recognizing an opportunity to rid Joseon of Qing influence and gain full control of the country for itself. Kim, unaware of this, trusted Japan and pressed on with his preparations.

Finally, on the day of a banquet to celebrate the opening of Joseon's new Postal Administration, the progressives made their move. Since the calendar name for 1884 was *gapsin*, the incident became known as the Gapsin Coup.

A banquet becomes a bloodbath

The Postal Administration, Korea's first postal service, opened on December 4, 1884 (October 17 according to the lunar calendar). On the same day, a banquet was held to celebrate. In attendance were many of the country's top officials and various foreign diplomats.

Chaos at the Postal Administration banquet
The foreigners and Joseon officials at the party were startled at the sight of Min Yeongik slumped on the floor and bleeding. They had no idea they were witnessing the beginning of a coup.

At ten o'clock that night, just when the party had reached full swing, somebody shouted: "Fire!" Min Yeongik, whose status as a relative of Queen Min made him one of the most powerful men in the country, ran outside the building. Shortly afterwards, he staggered back inside, bleeding, and collapsed. He had been stabbed in an ambush by members of the progressive faction. The party descended into chaos as its guests began to flee. This was the first act of the Gapsin Coup.

After eliminating Min and other members of the conservative faction at the Postal Administration, Kim Okgyun ran over to Changdeokgung Palace to find King Gojong. He now delivered a carefully prepared lie:

"Qing forces are rebelling, setting fire to the palace and killing ministers! You must flee immediately!"

Just then, a loud explosion shook the earth. Kim urged the startled king once again to flee and take refuge in Gyeongugung Palace, telling him he must request a military escort from the Japanese legation because of the danger he faced. Confused by the ongoing explosions nearby, Gojong hurriedly sent a letter to the Japanese legation requesting help. When the king and queen reached Gyeongugung, they were surrounded by 200 Japanese troops led by minister Takezoe.

Dawn arrived. The progressives announced that they would be forming a new government. The positions of chief and second state councillor, respectively, would be filled by Yi Jaewon (nephew of the Daewongun) and Hong Yeongsik; Seo Gwangbeom would be in charge of foreign affairs; Park Yeonghyo and Seo Jaepil in charge of military affairs; and Kim Okgyun vice minister of taxation. The whole country was now effectively in progressive hands. Feeling elated, Kim Okgyun handed King Gojong a reform plan outlining the policies that would now be introduced.

On the third day after the coup, Gojong returned to Changdeokgung and told the progressives that he would implement their reforms. Kim now believed Joseon was set on the path they had intended, and was destined to become a new country.

Just then, more explosions rang out and Qing troops burst into the palace. Realizing the situation had turned against

'Godaesu': court lady and coup conspirator

The booming explosions that rocked Changdeokgung while Kim Okgyun was lying to Gojong about Qing forces storming the palace were all part of the plan. Gunpowder was placed in bamboo stems in advance, ready to be lit at the appointed time. This part of the plot was carried out by a court lady named Godaesu.

Godaesu was a nickname that reflected the way its bearer was very strong, and ugly enough to turn heads. She was a *musuri*, the lowest rank among court ladies, who were already of low status. This meant she spent her days doing tasks like fetching water and washing clothes. So how did she come to take part in the progressives' coup? Kim Okgyun mentions her just once in his book *Gapsin illok* ("Journal of 1884"):

"Court lady X (42 years old. Burly in build and strong enough to fight five or six men at once, hence the nickname 'Godaesu.' Is a favorite of the queen and spends time close to her. Has provided us with occasional inside information for the last ten years.) filled some bamboo stems with gunpowder, kept them at the ready, then ignited them at the sight of the fire outside, a prearranged signal."

them, the Japanese troops guarding Gojong beat a hasty retreat. This was a big setback for the progressives, who had placed all their trust in the Japanese army. There was little they could do now but run away. Nine of them, including Kim Okgyun, Park Yeonghyo, Seo Gwangbeom and Seo Jaepil, fled to the Japanese legation, from where they were later smuggled to Incheon in wooden crates and loaded onto a ship bound for Japan.

Postal Administration building
This was the headquarters of Korea's first ever postal service. It now stands quietly in Seoul's Jongno-gu district, having seemingly forgotten the frantic events of 1884.

Members of the progressive faction who hadn't managed to flee were put to death along with their immediate families and even distant relatives. Kim Okgyun's mother and elder sister drank poison to kill themselves in order to avoid execution, while his wife, Lady Yu, and their daughter became slaves. The curtain thus fell on the Gapsin Coup, which had created a new state that lasted just three days. The reform plan the progressives had so painstakingly prepared, too, became a meaningless scrap of paper and eventually disappeared.

So why had Qing troops showed up at the critical moment? They had been called by Queen Min. While taking refuge in the palace, she had heard the news that her relatives and fellow conservatives were being killed and injured, and that the progressives had taken power. She then sent an urgent request to Qing for military help. The queen despised the

Park Yeonghyo's Taegeukgi
This Taegeukgi, an early version of today's South Korean flag, is said to have been created on a ship bound for Japan in 1882 by Park Yeonghyo, who had been sent as a Joseon envoy at the time. We used to have no way of knowing what Park's Taegeukgi looked like. Recently, though, a Taegeukgi thought to be the one drawn by him was discovered in the British National Archives. If you look closely, you'll see that it's different from today's national flag: its *taegeuk* is shaped differently and its *gwae* (quadrigrams) are in different positions. The Taegeukgi we use today was officially designed in 1949.

Meiji Maru This was the ship on which Park sailed to Japan.

progressive faction and was a supporter of the conservatives.

Why the Gapsin Coup failed

Why did the Gapsin Coup succeed for only three days?

Firstly, it didn't have the support of the people. Merchants and farmers were very hostile towards progressives at the time: the former were unable to sell enough goods because of their Japanese counterparts, while the latter were on the verge of bankruptcy as the Japanese took away all the rice they worked so hard to grow. There was no way they would support a faction that advocated working together with Japan and developing in the same way. Moreover, the progressives made no attempt to win commoners over to their side.

Secondly, the enlightenment faction relied excessively on Japan. Despite all their efforts to break free of Qing control, they failed to recognize Japan's true intentions and merely assumed that

Leaders of the Gapsin Coup
From left to right: Park Yeonghyo, Seo Gwangbeom, Seo Jaepil and Kim Okgyun. The members of the progressive faction died miserable deaths: one of them, Hong Yeongsik, along with Park Yeonggyo, the elder brother of Park Yeonghyo, vowed to stay with the king and was killed by Qing forces. Yu Honggi, hearing that the coup had failed, disappeared.

enlightenment meant being like Japan. When the Japanese army broke its promise to them by retreating, their plan soon collapsed.

Despite its flaws, the Gapsin Coup was Joseon's first reformist movement aimed at creating a modern state. The progressives' plan offers a glimpse of their bold intentions to eradicate various political and social ills.

What became of Kim Okgyun after he fled to Japan? He was treated very cooly—understandably, since all Japan had ever planned to do was use the progressives as a way of gaining total control of Joseon. For ten years, he traveled through various countries, unable to return to his homeland. Then, while staying at an inn in China, he was assassinated by Hong Jongu, a member of Joseon's conservative faction. Kim's body was returned to Joseon, where it received the further punishment of having its head cut off and hung up under a banner reading "Okgyun, a high traitor."

The Gapsin Coup reform plan
- Immediately repatriate the Daewongun, who was abducted to Qing during the Imo Incident; stop paying tribute to Qing and sever relations with it
- Abolish social caste divisions and hereditary privilege and appoint individuals based on merit
- Eradicate official corruption by reforming the land tax system in order to improve the lives of the people and the national economy
- Do away with the *hwangok* tax forever
- Severely punish those whose actions harm the state
- Abolish superfluous government offices
- Put the Ministry of Taxation in control of the national economy
- Select talented young people to be sent for education overseas
- Abolish the state examination system

The death of Kim Okgyun
Kim died in Shanghai in 1894 after being shot by conservative assassin Hong Jongu. The picture on the left is a Japanese illustration of the assassination; on the right is a portrait of Hong.
– University of Seoul Museum

Hong Jongu

A military uprising: The Imo Incident

Two years before the Gapsin Coup, a military uprising occurred. The affair is known today as the Imo Incident, after the year in which it took place. Why would soldiers revolt when they're supposed to defend the state?

The uprising was triggered by unpaid wages. But the more fundamental causes were opposition to Japan and anger at political corruption. At this time, the soldiers had not received their salaries for more than a year. They were supposed to be paid in rice, but there wasn't enough to give them because the commodity had been pouring out of Joseon since the signing of the Treaty of Ganghwa.

For a five-year period beginning the year after the signing of the treaty, rice had accounted for thirty percent of all Korean exports to Japan. You might think that high export volumes are a good thing, but the problem here was that rice was sold to the Japanese at very low prices. The empire's merchants made huge profits by buying cheap rice from Joseon and selling it at a big markup so that they, not the farmers, reaped the benefits of the export system. In fact, Joseon's high rice exports caused a domestic shortage that pushed up prices and made it even harder for poor Koreans to eat properly. As a result, the people of Joseon felt deep anger and resentment towards Japan.

One day in June 1882, word came that the soldiers were finally to be paid their overdue salaries. Happily, they ran to the Tribute Bureau to receive their rice. When they got there, however, a surprise awaited. The rice smelled musty and was mixed with large amounts of sand and chaff. The official in charge had siphoned off the rice for himself, then topped up the rest with sand. The

Byeolgigun soldier
The Imo Incident was the work of soldiers from an old-style army unit, rather than the Byeolgigun ("Special Skills Force"). The latter was a new type of unit, set up in line with progressive policies, that received modern-style training from Japanese instructors. Its men were much better paid than old-style forces, too.

soldiers' pent-up rage now erupted.

"Whether we starve or they execute us, we're dead men anyway!" one of them shouted. "We might as well get revenge in the process!"

The soldiers' anger was targeted at the Japanese, at corrupt officials and at the royal court for getting Japan involved in Korean affairs in the name of progress. They descended upon the Japanese legation, the tribute building and the home of Min Gyeomho, the head of the Tribute Bureau. Before long, poor inhabitants of areas around Wangsimni and Itaewon joined them.

The soldiers killed Yi Choeung, a government minister, and Min Gyeomho. They then headed to the palace to find Queen Min, whom they considered the source of all their problems, but she managed to slip away in disguise and flee to Janghowon. The terrified Japanese minister set fire to his own legation, creating a diversion, and managed to run away to Japan.

The soldiers wanted the Daewongun back in power. His refusal to compromise with outside forces and the fact that he wasn't a member of the corrupt Min faction made him their only hope. Thus it was that, after some ten years in the wilderness, the Daewongun took charge again. But it wasn't to last long this time. Qing now sent forces to abduct the reinstated regent. Then, in exchange for helping put Gojong and Min back in power, it persuaded Joseon to sign a treaty of commerce—titled "Joseon-Qing Regulations for Maritime and Overland Trade"—that would prove very profitable.

Japan refused to sit by while all this was going on, and demanded compensation for the damage to its legation. Joseon had no choice but to sign yet another treaty, which this time stipulated that it would pay 500,000 won in compensation and allow Japanese troops to be stationed on its soil. This new agreement is known as the Treaty of Chemulpo [Jemulpo], after the area of Incheon in which it was signed. Like the Treaty of Ganghwa-do, it worked entirely in Japan's favor.

The Imo Incident left Joseon even more dependent on Qing, setting the scene for the Gapsin Coup and its rejection of Chinese influence.

CHAPTER 12

Jeon Bongjun and the Donghak Peasant Revolution

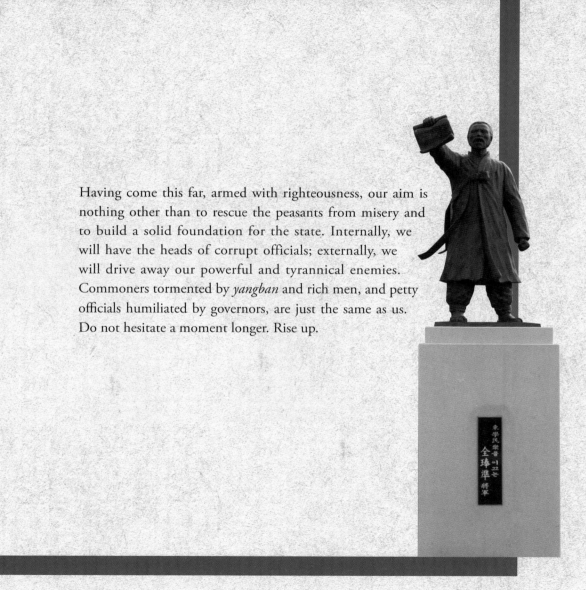

Having come this far, armed with righteousness, our aim is nothing other than to rescue the peasants from misery and to build a solid foundation for the state. Internally, we will have the heads of corrupt officials; externally, we will drive away our powerful and tyrannical enemies. Commoners tormented by *yangban* and rich men, and petty officials humiliated by governors, are just the same as us. Do not hesitate a moment longer. Rise up.

| TIME LINE | -------- (1864) -------- (1871) -------- (1876) ------------

Joseon period
Donghak leader Choe Jeu
executed

U.S. invasion
of Ganghwa-do

Treaty of Ganghwa signed
with Japan

You may have heard of a character in Korean history with the intriguing nickname, "General Mung Bean." Though he might sound like something out of a comic book, the general, whose real name was Jeon Bongjun, played a leading role in an event that shook Joseon to its very foundations: the Donghak Peasant Revolution.

Remember how I wrote in my last letter that Joseon faced two major tasks after opening its ports? One was to defend itself against outside powers, and the other was to achieve social reform.

The progressive faction that led the Gapsin Coup hoped to implement reform but ended up failing because of its reliance on Japan. And yangban *Confucian scholars who opposed the progressives tried to defend Joseon against foreign powers but were opposed to reform. Each side went after only one target, missing the other as a result.*

Now, a huge movement occurred that realized the importance of each task and attempted to solve them both. It was led neither by progressives nor Neo-Confucian scholars, but by the country's peasants. Today, it's known as the Donghak Peasant Revolution and it's what we'll be exploring in this letter.

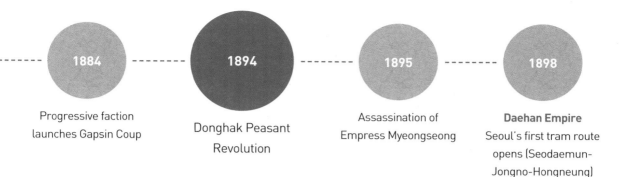

1884	1894	1895	1898
Progressive faction launches Gapsin Coup	Donghak Peasant Revolution	Assassination of Empress Myeongseong	**Daehan Empire** Seoul's first tram route opens (Seodaemun-Jongno-Hongneung)

The beginning of the revolution came in the form of an uprising by peasants in Gobu, Jeolla-do Province, who were no longer able to stand the tyranny of local magistrate Jo Byeonggap. It began on the morning of January

Manseokbo Memorial Stele Manseokbo was a reservoir that kicked off the Gobu peasant uprising. Local magistrate Jo Byeonggap built it even though there was already another reservoir, and began charging for the use of water. The peasants, no longer able to endure his corruption, staged an uprising and demolished Manseokbo. Today, all that remains of it is this stele in Ipyeong-myeon, Jeongeup, Jeollabuk-do Province.

Stele in remembrance of Jo Gyusun
Gobu governor Jo Byeonggap collected 1,000 *nyang* in taxes from local commoners in order to erect this stele in remembrance of his father. It stands in the grounds of Pihyangjeon, a famous pavilion in Taein-myeon, Jeongeup, Jeollabuk-do Province.

11, 1894, when the peasants, led by Jeon Bongjun, stormed the government office in Gobu. Overrunning the place with ease, they discovered that Jo had already fled. Jeon brought out the grain piled in the office storehouse and handed it to the starving peasants, then freed wrongfully detained prisoners from their cells.

As the news from Gobu spread across the country, a series of peasant armies sprang up in each region. Comrades of Jeon Bongjun such as Kim Gaenam, Son Hwajung, O Hayeong and Son Yeook all led peasant armies to join in the battle. The overall number of peasant forces swelled to some 13,000. Their army struck camp on Mt. Baeksan, which, despite not being all that high, offers a clear view across the surrounding plain in all directions. The mountain was soon

Donghak peasant army at Mt. Baeksan
This painting shows peasant soldiers and Jeon Bongjun gathered on Mt. Baeksan. Jeon is the figure standing resolutely in the center of the picture.

covered in white-clad peasant soldiers armed with bamboo spears. When they stood up, it turned completely white; when they sat down, it grew a forest of spears.

'Save the country and provide for the people'

The peasant army carried banners with the Chinese characters "輔國安民," meaning "save the country and provide for the people." This slogan neatly summed up the reasons for the uprising.

Jeon Bongjun, leader of the peasant army, published a text openly declaring what his forces would do next:

"Having come this far, armed with righteousness, our aim is nothing other than to rescue the peasants from misery and to build a solid foundation for the state. Internally, we will have the heads of corrupt officials; externally, we will drive away our powerful and tyrannical enemies. Commoners tormented by *yangban* and rich men, and petty officials humiliated by

House of Jeon Bongjun
This house in Jeongeup, Jeollabuk-do Province, is where Jeon once lived. Though he was of *yangban* status, his family was very poor. Jeon was a short man, which is how he acquired the nickname Nokdu, which means "mung bean." His courage and strength, however, are said to have been exceptional.

governors, are just the same as us. Do not hesitate a moment longer. Rise up. If you miss this chance, you will only be left with regret."

Jeon also announced four cast-iron rules of conduct for the peasant soldiers:

"Firstly, no indiscriminate killing of people or harming of livestock. Secondly, continue to serve your parents with loyalty while working to save the country and improve the lives of the people. Thirdly, drive out the Japanese barbarians and rectify the political situation. Fourthly, invade Hanyang by force and eliminate corrupt officials."

Let's take a closer look at Jeon Bongjun at this point. He studied Confucianism like any other *yangban*, worked as a village schoolmaster and even made his own medicine to treat others. At the same time, he was strongly aware of the need to solve Joseon's many problems and improve the lives of its people. To this end, he gathered a group of like-minded individuals that included Kim Gaenam and Son Hwajung. They made a solemn vow of solidarity.

At the time, most *yangban* regarded Donghak as a wicked ideology that was possessing the people, while the government had banned the religion altogether. Jeon, on

! The secret of Buddha's belly button

Half-way up the mountain that rises behind Seonunsa Temple in Gochang, Jeollabuk-do Province, is a huge image of the Buddha carved into a cliff face. According to legend, the belly button of the Buddha harbored a mysterious secret that, when revealed to the world, would lead to the downfall of Hanyang. Which meant, of course, the end of the Joseon Dynasty.

Just before the outbreak of the Donghak Peasant Revolution, a rumor went around that somebody had removed the secret. The person in question was said to have been Son Hwajung, one of the leaders of the peasant army. Hearing the rumor, the governor of Jeolla-do had some peasant

Seonunsa Dosolam Maaebul
Can you see the square shape near the Buddha's belly button? That's where they say the secret was hidden. The carving is located in Gochang, Jeollabuk-do Province.

soldiers arrested and interrogated, but nobody knew the whereabouts of the written secret. What was it that Son had pulled out from the belly button of the Buddha?

The answer is said to have been Silhak scholar Jeong Yagyong's *Gyeongse yupyo*. The story goes that there was a special edition of the book, different to the well-known version, that included the most important points of Jeong's reform program. This edition no longer survives, but it's highly likely that Jeon Bongjun was influenced by Jeong's thought.

Kim Gaenam (left) and Song Hwajung (right) Jeon Bongjun's fellow leaders were arrested and put to death after the defeat of the Donghak army.

the other hand, loved Donghak and had become a believer. He probably believed the Donghak conception of humans as one with heaven offered hope to the commoners who suffered from such discrimination in Joseon.

One day, Jeon was struck by tragedy when his father, Changhyeok, was flogged to death while attempting to stand up to Jo Byeonggap. This incident finally prompted Jeon into action. He now took a leading role in the Gobu peasants' uprising.

The first clash with government forces

In May, 1894, hearing news of the peasant uprising, the royal court hurriedly sent government troops with orders to put down the revolutionaries. The first clash took place at Hwangtojae, a foggy spot where rivers flow on three sides.

It was nighttime when the government troops reached Hwangtojae. Sure enough, they found themselves in thick fog. The peasant soldiers had slipped out of their camp and were hiding in the hills nearby, waiting. Unaware of this, the government troops descended upon the camp. Just when they realized it was empty, screaming peasants launched their attack. The government forces were wiped out in no time.

The battle of Hwangtojae
It was here that the peasant army won a resounding victory over government forces, filling it with confidence as it swept through each Jeolla-do county in turn.

When the fog lifted in the morning, Hwangtojae was littered with their bodies.

Emboldened by its victory, the peasant army rapidly gained control of each county in Jeollabuk-do—Jeongeup, Heungdeok, Gochang, Mujang, Yeonggwang, Hampyeong —eventually taking Jeonju, the most important city in the entire southwestern Honam region. On Pungnammun, the southern gate of Jeonju's city wall, is a sign that reads "湖南第一城," meaning "Honam's number one city;" it was this major hub that had fallen to the peasant army. News of this development came as a severe shock to the royal court in Hanyang. That Jeonju was also the location of Gyeonggijeon, the shrine that housed the portrait of Joseon founder Taejo Yi Seonggye, just made matters worse.

Sensing a crisis, the government adopted a conciliatory

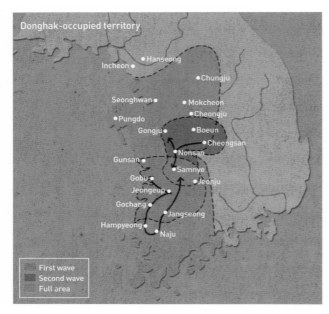

Donghak-occupied territory

Hanseong
Incheon
Chungju
Seonghwan
Mokcheon
Pungdo
Cheongju
Gongju
Boeun
Cheongsan
Nonsan
Gunsan
Samnye
Gobu
Jeonju
Jeongeup
Gochang
Jangseong
Hampyeong
Naju

First wave
Second wave
Full area

After taking Jeongeup, Heungdeok, Gochang, Mujang, Yeonggwang and Hampyeong in Jeolla-do Province, the peasant army finally captured Jeonju, the most important city in Honam. It now transformed the entire Jeolla-do region into a world of its own.

approach to the peasants and offered to hear their demands. Jeon now faced a dilemma: should he maintain the momentum of the uprising and press on towards Hanyang, or make peace?

Several thoughts passed through the Mung Bean General's mind: Would his army really be able to occupy Hanyang? Didn't his men need a rest after days of constant fighting? What would they do once they had taken the capital? And what about this rumor that Qing and Japan were going to have a war in Joseon, on the pretext of putting down the peasant revolution—could it really be true? And so on.

At this point, the Joseon government had already asked Qing for help with crushing the uprising, at a secret meeting between Tribute Bureau chief Min Yeongjun and Yuan Shikai, a Qing official in Joseon at the time. Asking another country for help with putting down your own people may seem outrageous today, but to the kind of elite that ruled Joseon at the time it was nothing. And it was exactly what Qing wanted to hear.

The situation now grew worse. Japan, hearing that Qing

Pungnammun is the southern gate of Jeonju's city wall. Jeonju was the most important city in the Honam region and the home of Gyeonggijeon, a shrine the housed the portrait of Joseon founder Yi Seonggye. When the peasant army took the city, the Joseon royal court was deeply shocked and sued for a truce. This resulted in the Jeonju Peace Treaty.

troops were on their way to Joseon, sent forces of its own. Before long, 1,500 Qing and 6,000 Japanese men arrived. Joseon was now a powder keg.

Down in Jeonju, Jeon Bongjun and the peasant army decided to make peace with the government on the condition that their reform plan be accepted. They believed driving out foreign forces from the country should now be the top priority. Representatives from both sides met in Jeonju and made the vow of peace that we now know as the Jeonju Peace Agreement.

Once the agreement was reached, the peasant soldiers

returned to their respective villages. But life didn't simply grind on as before: far from it. Now, every area in peasant army-controlled territory, which spanned Jeolla-do, Chungcheong-do and Gyeonggi-do provinces, had a "Local Directorate" that set about implementing the revolutionaries' reform plan with the participation of one of their representatives.

Not everything went smoothly for the Local Directorates. The peasants had long been oppressed by *yangban* and government officials, and sometimes their anger spilled over into violence. Some *yangban*, too, ended up losing it with the peasant army when the Local Directorates prevented

Local Directorates
These directorates occupy a very important place in Korean history, even though they were only established in Donghak-held areas. This was the first time that peasant representatives had participated in government for the sake of their own kind.

them from acting with the recklessness to which they were accustomed.

'Fight the Japanese to save the country'

Though the peasant army had disbanded after the Jeonju Peace Agreement, Japanese and Qing forces remained in Joseon. Japan now started a war, calculating that this was its chance to prise Joseon away from Qing for good. In June 1894, the conflict we now know as the First Sino-Japanese War broke out on territory that belonged to neither of the conflicting parties. The decisive battle of the war was fought in Pyeongyang, and won by Japan.

After its victory, Japan began controlling Joseon at will, with no resistance from the latter's royal court. When Jeon Bongjun heard about this, it seemed to him that the only option left was to gather the peasant army once again and drive out the intruders.

In September 1894, the peasant army finally rose up again. This time, its banners carried the slogan "抗日救國," meaning "fight the Japanese to save the country." Gathering in Nonsan, Chungcheongnam-

Japanese forces land at Jemulpo
When Qing sent troops to Joseon to put down the peasant revolution, Japan responded by landing forces of its own at Incheon. Joseon braced itself for imminent war.

do, the peasant soldiers prepared for war. They now fought a key battle with Japanese forces at Ugeumchi in Gongju.

Ugeumchi, also known as Gaegeumti, is a steep hill. As the peasant army climbed it, the Japanese opened fire with their state-of-the-art weapons. The bamboo spears and bare hands of the peasants were no match for the hail of bullets that met them. Gradually, Jeon's men lost ground. Their bodies piled up on the hill, with streams of blood flowing away between them.

The defeated peasant army pulled back to Nonsan, then to Jeonju. Regrouping, they fought battles at Wonpyeong and Taein but were beaten there, too. Jeon now lost all hope and ordered his men to disband. With three subordinates, he traveled to Sunchang to take refuge for a while and consider

Jeon Bongjun under arrest
This photo shows Jeon on his way to Seoul after being captured in Sunchang. The caption on the bottom right reads "Donghak ringleader Jeon Bongjun." Who might the photographer have been?

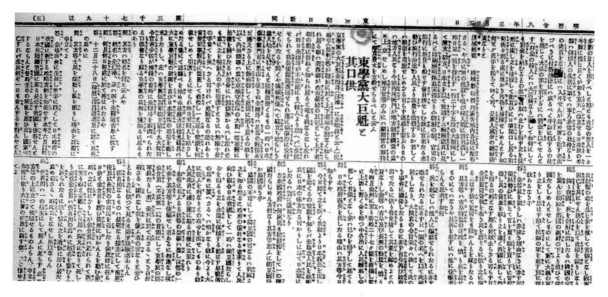

Record of Jeon Bongjun's interrogation
This document records the exchange between Jeon and his Japanese interrogator. It was published in a Japanese newspaper at the time. When asked about the reason for the uprising, Jeon answers: "How could the people live in peace if the country collapsed? ... I decided to tie my own fate to that of my country, and launch a rebellion."

his next move.

Jeon looked up Kim Gyeongcheon, an old friend who lived in Sunchang. But Kim, unable to resist the reward on the Mung Bean General's head, betrayed him. After seeing Jeon to bed for the night, he sent word to the local government office. Jeon barely had time to register the club that came out of the darkness and hit him on the head before he sank out of consciousness.

Following his arrest, Jeon was taken to Hanyang and held at the Japanese legation. His captors did their best to persuade him to plead unconditionally for his life, but Jeon cut them short:

"I've no intention of making such a pathetic choice."

After five rounds of interrogation, Jeon was sentenced to death and hanged. He was forty-one years old.

Donghak Peasant Revolution Centennial Tower
Built to commemorate the centenary of the 1894 revolution, this 18.94-meter tower is located in Jeon Bongjun Park at the entrance to Naejangsan National Park. You can almost hear the cries of the peasants all those years ago.

What made the general and his peasant soldiers fight so hard? What kind of future did they dream of? The revolutionaries wanted a world free from the clutches of corrupt officials, with no discrimination against peasants and *cheonmin*. They wanted a government that would stand up to the Japanese. Jeon Bongjun and the peasant army were out to reform Joseon society, rid it of foreign interference, and create better lives for its people.

In the end, their uprising failed and their dreams went

unfulfilled. But the seeds of hope that they sowed in the hearts of so many people never died. From then on, their memory was preserved in a song that was passed from one generation to the next:

"Bluebird, little bluebird! Don't land in the mung bean field! If the mung bean flowers fall, the mung bean jelly peddler will cry."

The attack on Gyeongbokgung and the Gabo Reforms

On the morning of June 25, 1894, some forty-five days after the Jeonju Peace Agreement was reached, gunfire-spraying Japanese troops attacked Gyeongbokgung. Threatening King Gojong, they forced him to appoint men of their choice to top government positions, then had him implement a series of reforms. These are known as the Gabo Reforms, after the calendar name of 1894. Needless to say, the reforms were aimed not at helping Joseon but at making it easier for Japan to control.

Despite being introduced through Japanese interference, the Gabo Reforms contained many changes that had long been called for by various Koreans, including the Donghak peasant army and the enlightenment faction. Why? Because these reforms were urgently needed in Joseon and could no longer be put off. The key elements of the Gabo Reforms were as follows:

Kim Hongjip Kim was prime minister at the time of the Gabo Reforms. These changes attempted to bring improvement in a variety of areas, but were introduced through Japanese interference.

- No more reliance on Qing; all official documents to be dated according to a "state foundation" calendar that begins with the founding year of Joseon in order to emphasize national independence
- Abolition of the state examination system; appointment of officials to be based on ability rather than family background
- Abolition of the guilt-by-association system; only criminals, not their families and relatives, to be punished
- Prohibition of marriage for males below the age of twenty and females below the age of sixteen
- Permission for widows to remarry at will
- Abolition of slavery
- Use of money as the sole medium of tax payment
- Standardization of weights and measures
- Permission for *yangban* to engage in commerce
- Separation of the administrative affairs of the royal family and the state
- Sending of bright young people overseas for academic and artistic education

CHAPTER 13

The death of Empress Myeongseong

In 1895, Empress Myeongseong was killed by Japanese assassins—a shocking and tragic event in international affairs.

But it also seems to me that our judgment of Myeongseong today may be somewhat biased because of the terrible way she met her end.

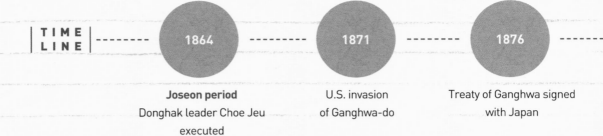

TIME LINE

1864

1871

1876

Joseon period
Donghak leader Choe Jeu
executed

U.S. invasion
of Ganghwa-do

Treaty of Ganghwa signed
with Japan

Today, Empress Myeongseong is one of the best-known figures in Korean history. Sadly, the notoriety of her assassination accounts for much of this fame.

Myeongseong was the wife of Gojong. I've mentioned her several times in previous letters, but under the name "Queen Min." So how did she go from being a queen to an empress?

This change came with the proclamation of the Daehan Empire in 1897, which meant that Gojong was now an emperor rather than a king. His wife, though she had died by this time, received a posthumous status upgrade to become an empress. So that's the title we'd better use from now on.

In 1895, Empress Myeongseong was killed by Japanese assassins—a shocking and tragic event in international affairs.

But it also seems to me that our judgment of Myeongseong today may be somewhat biased because of the terrible way she met her end. Though she is often viewed as a patriot who died heroically while trying to save her country from ruin, some also see her as a nasty daughter-in-law who elbowed her husband aside and then led the country to its downfall as she fought with his father, Heungseon Daewongun.

So which image is closer to reality? Let's find out more about Myeongseong, starting with her death.

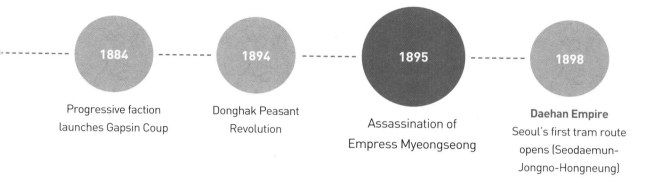

1884
Progressive faction launches Gapsin Coup

1894
Donghak Peasant Revolution

1895
Assassination of Empress Myeongseong

1898
Daehan Empire
Seoul's first tram route opens (Seodaemun-Jongno-Hongneung)

At around half past five on the morning of October 8, 1895 (August 20 by the lunar calendar), gunshots suddenly rang out at Gwanghwamun, the main gate of Gyeongbokgung Palace. Japanese attackers had forced their way in. Hong Gyehun, head of the Royal Guard unit guarding the palace, died on the spot from a gunshot wound. The raiders then hurried towards Gonnyeonghap, the empress's compound, which lay right at the back of the palace grounds.

The Okhoru affair

The assassins rushed into Okhoru, a building in the Gonnyeonghap compound, and dragged out several court ladies. This scene was witnessed by Afanasy Seredin-Sabatin, a Russian who had been secretly assigned to protect Gojong at the time. Here's how he described it:

"On the wooden verandah of Okhoru were twenty to twenty-five Japanese, armed with swords. They dragged the court ladies outside by their hair, threw them down into the courtyard and began kicking them."

Immediately after seeing this, Sabatin was taken away by the Japanese. Another testimony, provided by a palace court lady, was included in a report of the incident drafted by the American minister for his government:

"According to a court lady, she and her colleagues, startled by the commotion, crowded into the queen's room, along with minister Yi Gyeongjik, the director of the Royal Household Administration. Several Japanese forced their way into the room. Yi blocked the way to the queen, but was killed by a sword blow. The frightened queen claimed to be just a guest, and the other court ladies said the same, but one of the Japanese flung her to the ground, stamped on her chest three times and stabbed her with his sword. The other court ladies were also killed. It's clear that they were murdered to make sure that the queen was dead, since they all looked similar to her."

The court lady's account gives a very detailed description of the empress's last moments. It differs significantly from versions on television dramas, in which she foresees her own death and meets it with dignity. Perhaps the scriptwriter felt that someone of Myeongseong's status ought to show some degree of dignity.

After killing the queen, the Japanese set about destroying the evidence. Here's another eyewitness account, this time from a soldier:

"After the women had been killed, the head assassin took a photo out of his pocket and checked it. He then ordered his men to take two of the bodies outside. They poured kerosene on the bodies and set them alight. One of them was that of the queen. They did this in order to remove all traces of her."

The corpses were burned in Nogwon, a forest near Gonnyeonghap. Afterwards, the Japanese scattered the ashes in a pond. The other corpses are said to have been taken from the palace and dealt with in secret.

All of this happened within about an hour of the first gunshots by Gwanghwamun at half past five that morning. The event is now known as the assassination of Empress Myeongseong or, sometimes,

The assassination of Empress Myeongseong
The empress met a tragic death at the hands of Japanese assassins who stormed her quarters early one morning.

Okhoru
This building, the site of Empress Myeongseong's murder, is located in Geoncheongung, a complex right at the back of the grounds of Gyeongbokgung. It was recently restored.

Artist's reconstruction of Geoncheongung

Chwigyumun Gate

Jangandang Bukhaenggak

Gwanmyeongmun Gate

Boksudang Seohaenggak

Boksudang

Okhoru

Jangandang

Gonnyeonghap

Choyangmun Gate

Gonnyeonghap Namhaenggak

Gonnyeonghap Donghaenggak

as the Eulmi Incident, *eulmi* being the Korean calendar name for 1895.

The Japanese moved swiftly to deal with the aftermath of the incident. Minister Miura Goro had been drinking wine in the legation as he waited; when he received a report of the successful assassination, he immediately went to see Gojong in the palace and told him a lie:

"The Daewongun and the Korean royal guards have launched a revolt. The queen has fled and her whereabouts are currently unknown."

Gojong and the crown prince (later to become King

Gojong at the Russian legation
Gojong is the central of the three figures on the right, while Prince Sunjong is the young boy in the front on the left. Russia wielded huge influence and enjoyed many privileges in Joseon while the pair took refuge at its legation.

Sunjong) guessed that something bad had happened to the queen, but were surrounded by Japanese and could do nothing. After two days, it was announced that the queen had been stripped of her royal status and made a commoner; after five days, it was announced that her replacement would be chosen. Gojong wanted none of this, but was under duress and had to obey Japan's orders.

Gojong was now terrified that the Japanese would kill him at any moment. He refused to eat food prepared for him in the palace lest it be poisoned, having his meals cooked at the Russian or American legation instead and delivered in a locked case.

The anxious king now moved from Gyeongbokgung to Gyeongungung Palace (now known as Deoksugung). Shortly after this, he secretly fled to the Russian legation, which stood adjacent to Gyeongungung. Some even say there was a secret underground passageway that ran between the two.

Memorial to Empress Myeongseong
This stele, which commemorates the death of the empress, stands in front of the memorial hall at her birthplace in Yeoju, Gyeonggi-do Province.

Why the Russian legation, of all places? There were other options: the United States, France, or Britain, for example. Gojong chose Russia because it was Japan's most powerful rival at the time. He therefore believed the Russians would offer him the best protection against the nation they so disliked. The king and crown prince lived in the Russian legation for about a year, starting on February 11, 1896. For a monarch and crown prince to take refuge in a foreign legation on their own soil was something of a disgrace in international terms. But that was the reality Joseon faced.

Why did the Japanese kill Empress Myeongseong?

The empress's death at the hands of the Japanese was the product of the complicated international situation at the time. Tensions ran high between Japan, Qing and Russia, the three states that surrounded Joseon. Qing claimed that Joseon had long been its vassal state, while Russia wanted to use the kingdom to block Japan's growing influence in Asia. Japan, for its part, was hell-bent on gaining control of its western neighbor.

Having decided to get Qing out of the picture first, Japan started the First Sino-Japanese War. After winning the conflict, it forced Qing to abandon all claims to Joseon and went a step further by taking the Liaodong Peninsula for itself. This prompted Russia, worried that Japan was becoming too powerful, to take action.

Forming a diplomatic alliance with Germany and France in a move known as the Triple Intervention, Russia put pressure on Japan to return the Liaodong Peninsula to Qing.

No one was happier at the news of the Triple Intervention than Empress Myeongseong, who despised Japan in the belief that it was trying to exclude her and Gojong from politics and relegate them to figurehead status. In her view, Russia was now the only country that Joseon could rely on, given the weakened state of Qing. As soon as she heard about the Triple Intervention, the queen filled key government positions with members of Joseon's pro-Russian faction.

Angered at this turn of events, Japan searched desperately

The assassins
The men who killed Empress Myeongseong were more than just gangsters or assassins. Their leader, Shiba Shiro, had studied economics at Harvard and Pennsylvania universities. Horiguchi Kumaichi, meanwhile, was a law graduate from Tokyo Imperial University who went on to serve as Japan's minister in Brazil and Romania. Other figures involved included staff from the Japanese legation, policemen, soldiers and even newspaper reporters. The latter's duty was to cover the incident from angles that would work to Japan's advantage.

Area around the
Japanese legation
Japan was the first foreign
country to open a legation
in Hanyang. It was followed
by America, Britain,
France and Germany in
succession.

for ways to stop Joseon getting too close to Russia. It believed itself still too weak to take on Russia in another conflict like the recent Sino-Japanese war. The solution it now came up with was to get rid of Empress Myeongseong, Joseon's foremost pro-Russian figure. Charged with this task, minister Miura traveled to Joseon, where he devised an elaborate strategy that he named "Fox Hunt." Then, in accordance with the plan, he had the empress killed.

Afterwards, Miura, the assassins and forty-seven other people connected to the incident were summoned back to Japan and put on trial. This was nothing more than a perfunctory gesture, however, designed to quell international condemnation of government-sanctioned regicide. The trial concluded with all forty-seven defendants acquitted on grounds of insufficient evidence. The case of Empress Myeongseong's murder went unsolved, and remains shrouded in mystery.

Empress Myeongseong's funeral procession
The death of the empress was only officially announced two months after it had taken place. Her funeral was held two years later, in November 1897. This image, included in a *uigwe*, shows her funeral procession.
– Kyujanggak Institute of Korean Studies

The fact is, however, that the murder of the empress was committed by Japan in the midst of its struggle with the Western powers. The only thing missing is solid evidence.

The true face of Myeongseong

What did the empress look like? Some claim that the photograph generally claimed to be of her is actually of a court lady, and that an image that appears in *Dongnip jeongsin* ("The Spirit of Independence"), a book written by Syngman Rhee and published in San Francisco in 1910, shows the real empress. We still have no way of knowing which photo is genuine, however. Now, without a single authenticated photo of Myeongseong, all we can do is try and imagine how she might have looked, based on the accounts of those who actually met her.

Park Yeonghyo, a leading member of the progressive faction and son-in-law of King Cheoljong, gave the following description:

"She was not particularly tall, but not short by the standards of Joseon ladies either. She was slim in build and had a slender face too. Her eyes were narrow with upturned corners: not a gentle face at first glance, but then not a hard face either. It was fairly expressive for a Joseon lady, and she was quite pretty. As I recall, she had a scar from a boil, about an inch long, to the side of her forehead."

Meanwhile, Isabella Bird-Bishop, a British geographer who visited Joseon just before the empress's

Finding the real empress
1. Photo published in *Guksa* ("Korean History"), an early-1990s South Korean middle and high school textbook, as the likeness of Empress Myeongseong.
2. Image included in *Dongnip jeongsin* ("The Spirit of Independence"), written by the young Syngman Rhee.
3. Cover of *La Corée*, written by a French foreign correspondent in Qing at the time of the First Sino-Japanese War.
4. Photo made public by British collector Terry Bennett in 2006, with German caption reading "Die ermordete Königin" ("The murdered queen").

Until now, the first photo has been widely understood to be that of the empress, but I think it shows a court lady. No one knows for sure what Myeongseong really looked like.

assassination and met the royal couple no less than four times, remembered her in the book Korea and Neighbors as follows:

"Her Majesty, who was then past forty, was a very nice-looking slender woman, with glossy raven-black hair and a very pale skin, the pallor enhanced by the use of pearl powder. The eyes were cold and keen, and the general expression one of brilliant intelligence. ... As soon as she began to speak, and specially when she became interested in conversation, her face lighted up into something very like beauty."

Take these descriptions and see what your imagination can do with them—maybe you'll get an accurate idea of what Empress Myeongseong actually looked like.

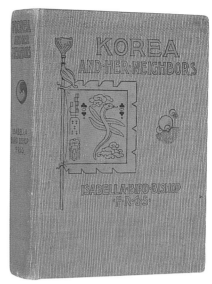

'Korea and Her Neighbors'
This book was written by British geographer Isabella Bird Bishop after five years' traveling in Joseon, beginning in 1894. Her travels included a month sailing up the Hangang River while observing the surrounding area, and extensive exploration on a pony. Several foreigners published Joseon travelogues at the time, but Bird Bishop's *Korea and Her Neighbors* is the most objective and detailed. It's a very good read.

Gojong's steadfast supporter

Empress Myeongseong was born in 1851. Hers was an illustrious family that had previously produced Queen Wongyeong, wife of King Taejong, and Queen Inhyeon, wife of King Sukjong. Her father did not reach a high position, but her grandfather was an official of junior second rank and served as deputy minister of personnel.

Hardly anything is known about Myeongseong's childhood. It's often said that she lost both parents at a young age

Gamgodang, former home of Empress Myeongseong
Myeongseong lived here from the time she left Yeoju for Hanyang, at the age of about eight, to the time she was chosen to be Gojong's queen. Gamgodang was also formerly the home of Inhyeon, queen of King Sukjong. Originally located in Seoul's Anguk-dong neighborhood, it was recently moved and rebuilt in Yeoju, next to the house where Myeongseong was born.

and went to live with relatives in Hanyang, and that the Daewongun chose her to marry his son because she was a lonely orphan. But this is not the case.

Myeongseong was not orphaned and did not go to live with relatives. Her father died when she was around eight years old, but her mother lived until 1874, some ten years after Myeongseong became queen. The young future queen lived with her mother in the same house that had once been home to Queen Inhyeon. So it seems unlikely that the Daewongun would have picked her on the grounds that she was an orphan.

Ten years after becoming king, Gojong finally pushed his father aside and began ruling Joseon himself. In need of new personnel to follow and support him, he filled most key government positions with his wife's relatives: the Min family.

For the next twenty years or so, until her assassination, the government was dominated by members of the Min faction, headed by Myeongseong herself. Gojong's most steadfast political ally was therefore also his wife.

A letter from Myeongseong in Hangeul

Empress Myeongseong often wrote letters in Hangeul to her relatives. Let's look at one she sent to Min Eungsik's son, Byeongseung, between July and September, according to the lunar calendar, 1894, around a year before her assassination.

It was Min Eungsik who had saved Myeongseong during the Imo Incident two years earlier, evacuating her from the capital to his house in Janghowon. When Min was sent into exile, Myeongseong sent his family letters of consolation. Here's an extract from one she wrote to his son, Byeongseung:

"I'll keep this short - recent events have been so terrible, too much to write here. What

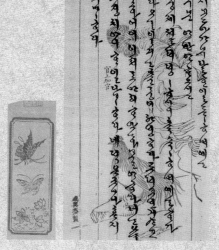

Letter written in Hangeul by Empress Myeongseong
The empress sent this letter to her nephew, Min Yeongso. On the left is a light pink-colored envelope decorated with butterflies.

happened to your father was awful. He hasn't forgotten about you - he asked how you were. It's good that he's not ill or injured, but still, my heart aches for him when I think what he must be going through. Here, the king is so worried that he cannot go about his daily duties properly, and the same goes for the crown prince. Everyone is on edge."-From "Myeongseong Hwanghu Min Bi Chinpil Milseo" ("Confidential Handwritten Letters by Empress Myeongseong") by Jeong Byeong-uk

Birthplace of Empress Myeongseong
This house in Yeoju, Gyeonggi-do Province, is where Myeongseong was born and spent her early childhood. The original buildings were burned down by the Donghak peasant army; the current rebuild dates from 1995. Myeongseong left this house and moved to Hanyang when she was around eight years old.

Empress Myeongseong as judged by history

Many negative portrayals of Myeongseong are the work of Japanese historians and contain plenty of exaggerations. Still, I'm not sure it's right to depict her as a thoroughly wonderful person either. Shouldn't our conclusion be based on a balanced assessment of the policies introduced during the twenty years for which she was an influential politician, and their outcomes? This period, from 1873 until 1895, was a very important chapter in Korean history. It saw a heady mixture of Western interference, existential threats to the Joseon Dynasty and movements demanding change, producing a string of events such as the Imo Incident, the Gapsin Coup and the Donghak Peasant Revolution. While the Daewongun responded to these circumstances with a closed-door policy, Myeongseong chose to open the country.

The major task facing Joseon as it opened its ports was that of autonomous modernization. The kingdom had to embrace Western culture, become stronger and develop its industry while stripping away outdated systems and establishing a new order.

Yet Myeongseong and the Min faction failed to do any of these things. As a result, they were supported by no one. The rebelling soldiers of the Imo Incident were out to get Myeongseong, while the progressives behind the Gapsin Coup and the peasant army of the Donghak Revolution all called for her overthrow and that of her clan. With no Korean allies left, Myeongseong ended up relying on Qing, then on Russia.

Empress Myeongseong was clearly an exceptional character. But her interests lay far from the autonomous modernization of Joseon, or the desires of its people. What she sought was a way to protect the royal family, including herself. Who knows—maybe she really did think that was what saving the country meant. That's as far as my assessment of Myeongseong's role in history goes. I wonder what you think.

'Tangang guri' stele
This stele was erected in 1905 to mark the former site of the house in which Empress Myeongseong was born. Its inscription reads "明成皇后誕降舊里," meaning "Old village where Empress Myeongseong came into the world." On the reverse of the stele is another inscription, said to be in the handwriting of Myeongseong's son, Emperor Sunjong.

The Daehan Empire is born

After Empress Myeongseong's assassination, Gojong sheltered in the Russian legation, with no thought of going back to his palace. But in February 1897, faced with a barrage of appeals from ministers for his return, he reluctantly moved back to Gyeongungung after about a year with the Russians. In October of the same year, the king changed the name of his country to Daehan ("Great Korea") and held a ceremony to have himself crowned as its

Wongudan Altar and Hwanggungu Shrine Wongudan was built by Gojong, who held his imperial coronation ceremony there. Within the Chinese cultural sphere, an altar like this was the symbol of an emperor, since no king was allowed to conduct rites there. This photo was taken in the early 1900s.

emperor. He announced that Daehan was an empire, no longer a vassal state of Qing but an independent state of equal status to its giant western neighbor, ruled by its own emperor. The Daehan Empire abandoned Qing era names and created a new era called Gwangmu. A new constitution, the "*Daehanguk gukje*" ("Daehan National System") was announced, the first article of which reads as follows:

"Daehan is an independent empire, as recognized by the other countries of the world."

Gojong, now an emperor, worked hard to illustrate his grandeur. He granted his queen, who had died such a wretched death at the hands of the Japanese, the posthumous title of "empress" and held a magnificent funeral for her. He remodeled the tombs and altars of his ancestors. And he built a second capital at Seogyeong (today's Pyeongyang), claiming that one capital was not sufficient for an empire.

The emperor promulgated a series of reforms under the slogan "consult the new while building on the foundations of the old." A national land survey was conducted and a business school established to promote industrial development.

The Daehan Empire existed for thirteen years, from its founding in 1897 to the signing of the Japan–Korea Annexation Treaty in 1910, when the latter became a colony of the former. This short period was probably Korea's last chance to build a modern, autonomous state. Unfortunately, however, the Daehan Empire proved incapable of holding off Japan's aggression.

Hwanggungu This shrine was located in the Wongudan Altar complex, an architectural manifestation of the Daehan Empire built to house ancestral tablets. Today only Hwanggungu remains, while the Westin Chosun Hotel stands on the former site of Wongudan. The shrine is located in the Sogong-dong neighborhood of Seoul's Jung-gu District.

Stone drums These drums were erected in 1902, to commemorate the fortieth anniversary of Gojong's coronation. Magnificent dragon motifs are carved on their sides. They sit in front of Hwanggungu.

CHAPTER 14

Treaty ports usher in the winds of change

Trams were an instant hit when they appeared on the streets of the capital. Some people made the trip from the countryside just to travel on the amazing new contraptions; others enjoyed the ride so much that they couldn't bear to get off until they had been from one end of the line to the other and back, several times. In the most serious cases, some people gave up their jobs altogether and devoted themselves to riding the trams until they had run through all their savings.

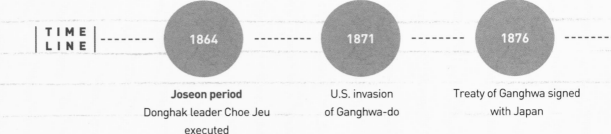

TIME
LINE

1864

Joseon period
Donghak leader Choe Jeu
executed

1871

U.S. invasion
of Ganghwa-do

1876

Treaty of Ganghwa signed
with Japan

How on earth did we ever get by without smartphones? These days they seem to have become an inseparable part of our lives. Remember the excitement you felt the first time you picked one up?

New technology has been surprising us for generations. People centuries ago must have been just as astonished as we are today when the latest inventions were revealed.

About a hundred years ago, new and amazing technology was pouring thick and fast into Joseon. Things that people had been using for longer than anyone could remember began disappearing, their places taken by all kinds of unfamiliar objects and devices.

Candles yielded to oil lamps; flints were replaced by matches.

Women went wild for face cream, a new Western arrival known as gurimu.

The opening of Joseon's ports brought breathtaking change to the lives of its people. Let's go back 100 years and see just what was going on.

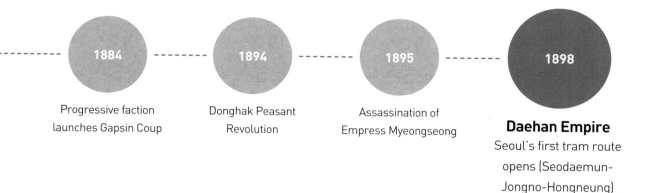

1884
Progressive faction
launches Gapsin Coup

1894
Donghak Peasant
Revolution

1895
Assassination of
Empress Myeongseong

1898
Daehan Empire
Seoul's first tram route
opens (Seodaemun-
Jongno-Hongneung)

Of all the change that rushed in via Joseon's newly opened ports, electricity must have been the most remarkable. It's so ubiquitous now that we take it utterly for granted, but in those days it was enough to make people giddy with excitement. Until then, sunset had meant lighting candles or oil lamps to see in the dark, but now electricity brought the gift of dazzling light even at night. And that

The first electric light
Joseon's first ever electric light was switched on at Gyeongbokgung on March 6, 1887. The ministers and court ladies who had gathered to watch were speechless. How must they have felt, seeing something so unimaginable for the first time?

The pond at Hyangwonjeong Pavilion This pond is located in the grounds of Gyeongbokgung Palace; the pavilion on an island in the center is called Hyangwonjeong. The first electric light in Joseon was powered by a hydroelectric generator that used water drawn from the pond. The light was therefore known as the "*mulbul*" ("water light"). Another name for it was "*myohwa*" ("peculiar fire").

wasn't all: it also powered yet more incredible inventions, like trams and telephones.

Electric lights, trams and telephones

Joseon's first electric light blinked into life in 1887, around ten years after the country began opening its ports. The light in question was located at Gyeongbokgung, near the sleeping quarters of King Gojong and Queen Min, and powered by water taken from the pond around Hyangwonjeong Pavilion to turn a generator.

This light seems not to have worked particularly well. Its tendency to keep flickering off and on again earned it the nickname *geondalbul*, which means "good-for-nothing light." Still, they say the king and queen used to turn on the good-for-nothing light and play around all night. This caused the water in the pond to overheat from constantly powering the generator, killing the fish in it en-masse. Gojong was eventually forced to get rid of the light. But three years later, in 1890, Jongno, one of Seoul's major thoroughfares, found itself illuminated by electric lighting.

No less amazing were trams—you may have seen them on television dramas, or even ridden them in some cities. The first trams in Hanyang ran on electricity, like the subways we use today, but above the ground and considerably slower.

The last one disappeared around 1970, but I still remember the sound of their bells ringing from when I was young.

Trams were an instant hit when they appeared on the streets of the capital. Some people made the trip from the countryside just to travel on the amazing new contraptions; others enjoyed the ride so much that they couldn't bear to get off until they had been from one end of the line to the other and back, several times. In the most serious cases, some people gave up their jobs altogether and devoted themselves to riding the trams until they had run through all their savings.

About a week after the tram service went into operation, a young child was run over and killed. This was Joseon's first ever traffic accident. At a time when the only other means of transport were palanquins and rickshaws, trams were the fastest things on the road. The tram driver at the time, who was Japanese, simply carried on: it was, in today's terms, a hit-and-run incident. Those in the street who had witnessed the accident were enraged, setting fire to the tram and descending upon the headquarters of the electricity company to protest.

A lot of people were less than happy with the introduction of the trams. Rickshaw

Korea-America Electric Company
Korea's first electric company opened near Dongdaemun Gate in January, 1898. Its original name was Hansung Electric Company, which was later changed to Korea-America Electric Company. Today it's known as KEPCO, an acronym for "Korea Electric Power Corporation."

Riding the tram
Seoul's first tram service was launched in May, 1898, running a west-east route across central Seoul from Seodaemun to Hongneung via Jongno. Gojong sometimes took the tram to visit the grave of Empress Myeongseong, who was buried at Hongneung. A south-north route, running from Yongsan up to Jongno via Namdaemun, opened the next year, followed by a third line, from Namdaemun to Seodaemun, in 1900.

Jongno around 1900
This is what a busy Seoul street looked like about 100 years ago. Young looked children are marveling at a passing tram, while rickshaw drivers hurry along, competing with the new mode of transport. Women are using parasols now, instead of traditional *sseugaechima* headdresses.

drivers hated the new mode of transport for taking away their customers, to the point where some of them tried to stop it from running. Others resented trams on the grounds that their power cables prevented rain, or that the power plant was built on land that resembled a dragon's back, which had caused a drought.

Four months after the first trams rolled into action, Joseon's first railway opened. The line ran from Incheon to Noryangjin, on the southern bank of the Hangang River. This new arrival was even bigger and faster than a tram. Foreigners coming off boats in Incheon could now take the train to Noryangjin, leaving just a short journey north to Seoul.

Huge changes were afoot in maritime transport, too. A ship now plied the route from Jemulpo, in Incheon, to the mouth of the Daedonggang River near Pyeongyang once a week, while steamers carried cargo up and down the Nakdonggang River in the southeast of the country.

What about telephones? The first system, a public network that reached outside the capital, was installed in 1902. But talking into a machine was such a strange and awkward sensation that the people of Joseon took quite a while to warm to these new devices. How could anyone maintain an air of respectability while holding a "telephone?" And how rude it was to make a phone call to somebody older because you were too lazy to make a proper visit! Some people who picked up a telephone when it was out of order and heard a series of mysterious clicks and beeping sounds would refuse to go near one ever again, believing the machines to be possessed.

Rickshaw driver and passenger

Locomotive on Korea's first railway The first train route, running from Incheon to Noryangjin in Seoul, opened on September 18, 1899. This photo shows an American Brooks locomotive.

In fact, there was a more fundamental reason for the unpopularity of telephones. Life in those days was much less busy and complicated, and people simply didn't need them all that often. It took another twenty or thirty years before the telephone was fully embraced by Korean society.

Western clothes, Western houses and coffee

Huge change occurred in the world of fashion, too: Western clothing had arrived. To a nation where people had previously

Telephone exchange Operators busy at work in 1902.

worn *hanbok* clothing all year round, Western fashion came as something of a novelty, if not a shock.

Still more upsetting, however, was the "top-knot edict" of 1895, which decreed that all men must cut off their traditional top-knots on the grounds of "hygiene benefits and convenience in everyday life." This caused a nationwide uproar, as the top-knot was a symbol of both marital status and Confucian culture. Though Gojong himself set an example by cutting off his top-knot, Confucian scholars resolutely opposed the decree. This coerced act was something that would make them resemble barbarians or Japanese.

"Our bodies and hair are inherited from our parents," they insisted. "We have no right to just cut them up at will."

Eventually, the country's scholars formed righteous armies and revolted. "They can chop off my head if they want," said one of them, Choe Ikhyeon, "but not my top-knot." Surprised by the strength of opposition to the decree, Gojong now announced that the men of Joseon were free to choose what they did with their top-knots.

As time went by, the number of people opting for short hair slowly increased. This was accompanied by a steady growth in the popularity of Western clothing, which looked much better with short hairstyles.

What about architecture? At first, people would buy Korean *hanok* houses, which were relatively easy

The top-knot decree
In 1895, the government issued a decree stating that all men in the country must cut off their top-knots. Confucian scholars strongly resisted the move, submitting petitions and forming righteous armies in revolt.

to afford, and decorate the interiors in Western styles, with carpets on the floors and fancy wallpaper. They were doing what you and I would call "conversions." Later, so-called *yangokjip* (literally "Western-roofed houses"), buildings with Western-style exteriors as well as interiors, began appearing.

Korea's first Western-style building
This dormitory for employees of German firm Meyer & Co. appeared in Incheon in 1884. With shapely arches and a long row of columns, it was a beautiful structure.

The first *yangokjip* building to appear in Korea was a dormitory for the workers of Meyer & Co., a German company. Built in Incheon in 1884, it was an attractive brick structure with a red-tiled roof. Another eye-catching building was the house of Yi Junyong, the grandson of Heungseon Daewongun, which amazed people with its Western-style indoor fireplaces, magnificent chandeliers, and window curtains. Japanese-style houses began appearing, too, especially in Namchon ("South Village"), the neighborhood to the south of Cheonggyecheon Stream.

When it came to Western food and drink, coffee proved extremely popular. Gojong was a great coffee lover: he is said to have begun drinking it while sheltering at the Russian legation following the assassination of Empress Myeongseong by the Japanese. A Western-style building called Jeonggwanheon Pavilion still stands in the grounds of Gyeongungung (now

General store advertisement
Run in a newspaper, this store ad shows a range of stylish products including business hats, sports hats, shoes, glasses and handbags.

named Deoksugung) Palace. It looks a bit like the more elegant cafés you see today. From time to time, Gojong would drink coffee there while listening to music.

The new fashions, architecture, food and drink were accompanied by changing customs. Particularly remarkable was the new style of wedding. Traditional ceremonies, conducted in the yard outside the home of the bride, with the bride and groom dressed in traditional robes and hats, were gradually replaced by Western-style weddings held in Christian churches. The spread of Christianity led to increasing numbers of new-style weddings in Protestant and Catholic churches—some were even held in Buddhist temples.

So when did the "wedding halls" you find all over Korea today, which specialize in hosting wedding ceremonies only, first appear? It was in the 1930s, around the same time that specialist wedding dress rental stores and makeup studios for brides began opening.

The introduction of Christian funerals brought sweeping change to traditional Korean ceremonies and ancestral rites, too. The Confucian custom of mourning the deaths of parents for three years and holding ancestral rites for the previous four generations of ancestors started gradually disappearing.

New-style wedding
This photo shows the wedding of Na Hyesok, a well-known early Korean Western-style painter. The groom wears a suit and the bride wears a veil, in the new style.

Wealth flows out the country

Surely developments like electricity, railways and modern shipping were a good thing? In themselves, perhaps. The problem was that these new things were owned not by Koreans but by foreigners, so that the profits they made disappeared overseas.

The countries that had signed treaties of commerce with Joseon took away the profits made from transportation, telecommunication and all kinds of natural resources. As a result, the resources that Joseon needed to develop its own economy gradually dried up, while the influx of well-developed businesses from abroad snuffed out nascent domestic industries. Japan, in particular, earned huge profits from Joseon, prompting one Korean newspaper, the *Dong-A ilbo*, to comment:

"Is Seoul for the people of Joseon or for the Japanese? The situation when it comes to telephones, a modern convenience, is lamentable. And that's not all. When it comes to all things modern—railways, steamers, paved roads, mail, telegraph networks—the people of Joseon provide the building costs and labor so the Japanese can make use of them. ... Today, we are not the masters of civilization but its slaves. People of Joseon, let us do all that we can to become the masters of civilization. If we can't, we might as well smash it up altogether."

While the citizens of Joseon enjoyed the sweet fruits of progress, using electricity and telephones, applying face cream and wearing Western clothing, the country's rice and gold were flowing overseas on trains and steamships. While most imports consisted of luxury goods, the bulk of exports comprised commodities like rice and soy beans.

! Joseon's first advertisement

The first advertisement to appear in Joseon was run by German trading company Meyer & Co. on February 22, 1886 in the fourth edition of weekly newspaper *Hanseong jubo*. Written in classical Chinese, it read as follows:

"Meyer & Co. has opened for business in Joseon. ... We sell alarm clocks, music boxes, amber, glass, and Western buttons, at reasonable prices, so please come and visit us. ... All customers, including children and the elderly, are guaranteed honest service."

Hangeul advertisements appeared mainly in the *Dongnip sinmun* ("The Independent") newspaper.

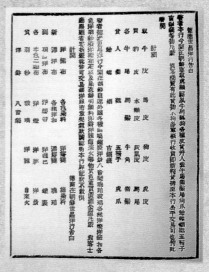

Advertisement Meyer & Co. in Hanseong jubo

Here's one for English dictionaries that appeared in the paper's first ever issue:

"Korean-English Dictionary and Korean-English Grammar: Nothing is more useful to Koreans trying to learn English. ... You need these books if you want to learn English in detail. Korean-English Dictionary is priced at 4 *won* and Korean-English Grammar at 3 *won*. Come and buy them at the Hanmihwa Printing House at Baejae Hakdang."

Japanese merchants made huge profits by buying cheap Korean rice and selling it in Japan at several times the price. In Joseon this created a shortage, causing local rice prices to skyrocket. Landowners grew wealthier, while the tenant farmers working their land grew poorer. The former were able to store the rice they received as rent and sell it for large profits when prices rose, but the latter had to forfeit much of what they harvested as rent, and were forced to pay high prices for more rice just to feed their own families.

"What good is it to us if we have a bumper harvest this year?" they sighed. "The Japs will scoop it all up anyway, pushing prices sky high and leaving us hungry as usual."

In his book *Maecheon yarok* ("Unofficial Records from Maecheon"), Confucian scholar Hwang Hyeon gave his own account of the situation:

"The people of our country are so dumb—it's awful. The only things coming in are strange or unnecessary items like silk, watches and paint, while the things leaving are what would normally be considered highly valuable: rice, soy beans, leather, gold and silver. Surely this can only lead the country to ruin?"

Incheon Port This photo shows Korean rice arriving at a dock in Incheon, whence it was taken by ship to Japan.

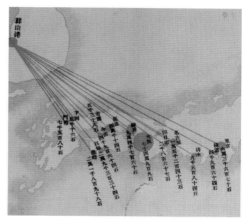

Rice exports from Gunsan to Japan (1926) Korean rice was taken to various cities in Japan, including 63,670 *seok* to Tokyo and 740,909 *seok* to Osaka. One *seok* is equivalent to roughly 180 liters.

When did Korea start using the solar calendar?

When Koreans tell each other their birthdays, they often specify whether they're using the solar calendar or the lunar calendar. The latter has been used in Korea since ancient times to calculate dates, while the former has only been part of life in the country for 100 years or so. On November 17 of the year 504 (the 504th year since the founding of Joseon), Korea switched to the solar calendar. It was now January 1, 1896.

The seven-day week and the division of each day into twenty-four hours began almost simultaneously with the introduction of the solar calendar. Before that, the days were divided into twelve hours, while dividing the week into seven days had not even occurred to anyone.

It was with the solar calendar that hours acquired numbers. Previously, the twelve hours of the day were named after the animals of the Twelve Earthly Branches: *ja* (rat), *chuk* (ox), *in* (tiger), *myo* (rabbit), *jin* (dragon), *sa* (snake), *o* (horse), *mi* (sheep), *sin* (monkey), *yu* (rooster), *sul* (dog) and *hae* (pig). So the time might be "rat o'clock," or you might have to get to work by "dog o'clock." Like hours, years passed in cycles of the Twelve Heavenly Branches. Even today, most people know whether they were born in the year of the horse, or the rooster, or whenever. One clear difference between this system and a numerical one is that the former can carry all kinds of other connotations and characteristics—"people born in the year of the horse are extroverted," "people born in the year of the rat end up being wealthy," and so on—while the latter simply describes the order of years as time passes.

A lunar year is about eleven days shorter than a solar year. To make up for this, an extra "leap month" is added every two or three years. The "second February" of 1795, during which King Jeongjo held his grand procession to Hwaseong, was an example of this. Unlike the extra day inserted into the solar calendar every four years, which is always February 29, the lunar leap month is added to a different part of the year each time it occurs.

Once people started using the solar calendar instead of its lunar counterpart, dividing the day into twenty-four sections instead of twelve, and labelling segments of time with numbers instead of animal mnemonics, their concept of time itself began to change. The hours and years no longer had any particular preordained characteristics, and time became a commodity that belonged equally to everyone.

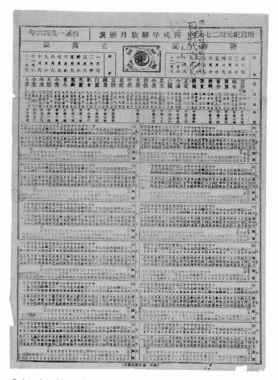

Calendar Nowadays nearly all states in the world use the solar calendar, but there was a time when each country had its own system. The Ancient Egyptians used a solar calendar, while the Sumerians and Chinese based theirs on the moon. Koreans, influenced by China, used the lunar calendar until 1896, after which they switched over. This photo shows a calendar published in 1946 by Jinmun Bookstore in Haman, Geongsangnam-do Province.
– National Folk Museum of Korea

Museum

Andong National University Museum — Letter from Yi Eungtae's wife 90

Bank of Korea Money Museum — Sangpyeongtongbo and Dangbaekjeon 165

Central Museum of Kyunghee University — Chunhyangjeondo 80

Chonbuk National University Museum — Jamae mungi 133

Dong-A University Museum — Sesipungsokdo 53

Independence Hall of Korea — Cheokhwabi 164 | Wang ocheonchukguk jeon 169 | Discussing the conquest of Korea 179 | Kim Okgyun's calligraphy 193 | Leaders of the Gapsin Coup 198

Jeju National Museum — Yinghuan zhilue 193

Jeonju National Museum — Stele in remembrance of Jo Gyusun 206

Konkuk University Museum — Yi family inheritance document 91

Korea University Museum — Preparing food 65 | Seoyu gyeonmun 183

National Folk Museum of Korea — Dipper 55 | Masks 76 | Folk paintings 78 | Wooden geese and nuptial cups 94 | Joseon cargo boat 129 | Mapae 132 | Calendar 257

National Museum of Korea — The Hwaseong Procession 15 | Plowing a field 57 | Cutting tobacco 58 | Jumak 62 | Yeollyeo Chunhyang sujeolga 70 | Chwihu ganhwa 83 | Hoehollyedo 87 | Dongguk daejeondo with the Baekdudaegan Range 108 | Honil gangni yeokdae gukdo jido 111 | Map section and woodblock 113 | Jeolla-do Mujanghyeondo 118 | Cheonhado 119 | Dongdaemun-oe Majangwon jeondo 119 | Susepae 128 | Harvesting rice 131 | Mapae 132 | Cheoksa yuneum 144 | Cotton armor 162

Map

Historical records and books

《정조실록(正祖實錄)》

《홍재전서(弘齋全書)》

《무예도보통지(武藝圖譜通志)》

유형원(柳馨遠), 《반계수록(磻溪隧錄)》

박지원(朴趾源), 《양반전(兩班傳)》

홍대용(洪大容), 《의산문답(醫山問答)》

정약용(丁若鏞), 《다산시문집(茶山詩文集)》

이익(李瀷), 《성호사설(星湖僿說)》

전순의(全循義), 홍기용·윤태순 공역, 《산가요록(山家要錄)》, 농촌진흥청, 2004

조수삼(趙秀三), 허경진 옮김, 《추재기이(秋齋紀異)》, 서해문집, 2008

이규상(李奎象), 민족문학사연구소 한문분과 옮김, 《18세기 조선 인물지 병세재언록(幷世才彦錄)》, 창작과비평사, 1997

유재건(劉在建) 엮음, 이상진 해역, 《이향견문록(里鄕見聞錄)》 하, 자유문고, 1996

서유영(徐有英), 김종권 교주(校註), 송정민 외 역, 《금계필담(錦溪筆談)》, 명문당, 2001

유희춘(柳希春), 이백순 역, 《미암일기(眉巖日記)》 1-5, 담양군, 2004

최한기(崔漢綺), 《청구도제(靑邱圖題)》

김정호(金正浩), 《동여도지서(東輿圖志序)》

조선총독부(朝鮮總督府), 《보통학교(普通學校) 조선어독본(朝鮮語讀本)》 5, 1934

《임술록(壬戌錄)》

《진양초변록(晉陽樵變錄)》

《진주초군작변등록(晉州樵軍作變謄錄)》, 진양문화원, 《진주목정사(晉州牧正史)》 3, 1994

정약용(丁若鏞), 이익성 옮김, 《經世遺表(경세유표)》 2, 한길사, 1997

정약용(丁若鏞), 다산연구회 역주, 《牧民心書(목민심서)》 2, 창작과비평사, 1979

최제우(崔濟愚), 《동경대전(東經大全)》, 해월최시형선생기념사업회, 1978

알렌, 김원모 완역, 《알렌의 일기》, 단국대학교출판부, 1991

최석우, 《한불관계자료 1846-1887》, 한국교회사연구소, 1986

유길준(兪吉濬), 채훈 역주, 《서유견문(西遊見聞)》, 명문당, 2003

김옥균(金玉均), 조일문 역주, 《갑신일록(甲申日錄)》, 건국대학교출판부, 1977

오지영(吳知泳), 이규태 교주, 《동학사(東學史)》, 1973

정병욱 교주, 명성황후 민비 친필밀서-언제면 군신(君臣)이 한자리에, 《문학사상》 1974. 10월호

Isabella Bird Bishop, *Korea and Her Neighbors: a narrative of travel, with an account of the recent vicissitudes and present position of the country 1,2*, London: John murray, 1898

황현(黃玹), 허경진 옮김, 《매천야록(梅泉野錄)》, 한양출판, 1995

조선왕조실록(朝鮮王朝實錄) http://sillok.history.go.kr

한국고전번역원 http://www.minchu.or.kr

한영우, 《정조의 화성행차 그 8일》, 효형출판, 1998

김영호, 《조선의 협객, 백동수》, 푸른역사, 2002

임동규, 《한국의 전통무예》, 학민사, 1990

한국실학연구회, 《한중실학사연구》, 민음사, 1998

유봉학, 《연암일파 북학사상 연구》, 일지사, 1995

강경원, 《이익》, 성균관대학교출판부, 2001

한국고문서학회, 《조선시대 생활사》 2, 역사비평사, 2000

황패강, 《조선왕조소설연구》, 단국대학교출판부, 1991

이민희, 《16~19세기 서적중개상과 소설·서적 유통관계 연구》, 역락, 2007

정노식, 《조선창극사》, 동문선, 1994

윤열수, 《민화 이야기》, 디자인하우스, 1995

김영학, 《민화》, 대원사, 1993

유홍준, 《문자도》, 대원사, 1993

장병인, 《조선전기 혼인제와 성차별》, 일지사, 1997

문숙자, 《조선시대 재산상속과 가족》, 경인문화사, 2004

최재석, 《한국가족제도사연구》, 일지사, 1983

Martina Deuchler, *The Confucian Transformation of Korea*, The President and Fellows of Harvard College, 이훈상 옮김, 《한국 사회의 유교적 변환》, 아카넷, 2003

Mark A. Peterson, *Korean Adoption and Inheritance: Case Studies in the Creation of a Classic Confucian Society*, Cornell East Asia Series no.80, East Asia Program, Cornell University, 1996, 김혜정 옮김, 《유교사회의 창출-조선중기 상속제와 입양제의 변화》, 일조각, 2000

이영춘, 《임윤지당-국역 윤지당 유고》, 혜안, 1998

이영춘, 《강정일당》, 가람기획, 2002

허경진, 《사대부 소대헌.호연재 부부의 한평생》, 푸른역사, 2003

망원한국사연구실 19세기 농민항쟁분과, 《1862년 농민항쟁》, 동녘, 1998

김준형, 《1862년 진주농민항쟁》, 지식산업사, 2001

윤석산, 《동학교조 수운 최제우》, 모시는사람들, 2004

한국역사연구회 19세기정치사 연구반, 《조선정치사 1800~1863》 상.하, 청년사, 1990

이태진, 《왕조의 유산 - 외규장각 도서를 찾아서》, 지식산업사, 1994

이광린, 《개화당연구》, 일조각, 1973

한철호, 《친미개화파연구》, 국학자료원, 1998

우윤, 《1894년: 갑오농민전쟁 최고 지도자, 전봉준》, 하늘아래, 2003

우윤, 《전봉준과 갑오농민전쟁》, 창작과비평사, 1993

한국역사연구회, 《1894년 농민전쟁연구 3 - 농민전쟁의 정치.사상적 배경》, 역사비평사, 1993

이태진, 《고종시대의 재조명》, 태학사, 2000

김윤희.이욱.홍준화, 《조선의 최후》, 다른세상, 2004

최문형 외, 《명성황후 시해사건》, 민음사, 1992

한영우, 《명성황후와 대한제국》, 효형출판, 2001

변원림, 《고종과 명성》, 국학자료원, 2002

나홍주, 《민비암살 비판》, 미래문화사, 1990

이기대 편저, 《명성황후 편지글》, 다운샘, 2007

문화의 창 총서 편집위원회 엮음, 《만국공원의 기억》, 인천문화재단, 2006

정구복.박광용.이영훈.최진옥.박연호, 《조선시대 연구사》, 한국정신문화연구원, 1999

국사편찬위원회, 《한국사》 34-35, 1995-1998

강만길, 《한국근대사》, 창작과비평사, 1984

젊은역사연구모임, 《영화처럼 읽는 한국사》, 명진출판, 1999

한국역사연구회, 《조선시대 사람들은 어떻게 살았을까》 1-2, 청년사, 1996

박한용.장원정.황경, 《시와 이야기가 있는 우리역사》 2, 동녘, 1996

한국역사연구회, 《우리는 지난 100년 동안 어떻게 살았을까》 1-3, 역사비평사, 1998-1999

전국역사교사모임, 《살아있는 한국사 교과서》 1-2, 휴머니스트, 2002

한국생활사박물관 편찬위원회, 《한국생활사박물관》 9-11, 2003-2004

이기백, 《신수판(新修版) 한국사신론》, 일조각, 1994

변태섭, 《한국사 통론(通論)》, 삼영사, 1986

한국역사연구회, 《한국역사》, 역사비평사, 1992

한국사특강편찬위원회 편, 《한국사 특강》, 서울대학교 출판부, 1990

한국역사연구회, 《한국사강의》, 한울아카데미, 1989

역사문제연구소, 《사진과 그림으로 보는 한국의 역사》 3, 웅진출판, 1993

구로역사연구소, 《바로 보는 우리 역사》 1, 1990

한국민중사연구회 편, 《한국민중사》 2, 풀빛, 1986

박은봉, 《한국사 상식 바로잡기》, 책과함께, 2007

박은봉, 《한권으로 보는 한국사 100장면》, 가람기획, 1993/ 《개정판 한국사 100장면》, 실천문학, 1997

박은봉, 《한국사 뒷이야기》, 실천문학, 1997

박은봉, 《세계사 뒷이야기》, 실천문학, 1994

박은봉, 《엄마의 역사편지》 2, 웅진주니어, 2000

Academic papers and essays

조광, 조선후기 실학사상의 연구동향과 전망, 《김창수교수화갑 기념사학논총》, 범우사, 1992

조광, 실학의 발전, 《한국사》 35, 국사편찬위원회, 1998

조광, 조선후기 사상계의 전환기적 특성-정학(正學).실학(實學).사 학(邪學)의 대립구도, 《한국사연구》 67, 1989

젊은역사연구모임, 희망과 절망이 공존하는 농촌, 《영화처럼 읽는 한국사》, 명진출판, 1999

이욱, 서울의 장사꾼들, 《조선시대 사람들은 어떻게 살았을 까》 1, 청년사, 1996

유필조, 장돌뱅이의 애환, 《조선시대 사람들은 어떻게 살았을 까》 1, 청년사, 1996

강명관, 조선후기 서적의 수입.유통과 장서가의 출현, 《민족문 학사연구》 9, 1996

안대회, 책장수 조신선; 세상의 책은 모두 내 것이니라, 《조선의 프로페셔널》, 2007

정재훈, 판소리는 과연 민중예술이었나, 《조선시대 사람들은 어떻게 살았을까》 1, 청년사, 1996

안대회, 천민 시인 이단전; "그래, 나는 종놈이다" 외친 천재문인, 《조선의 프로페셔널》, 2007

이순구, 조선초기 종법의 수용과 여성지위의 변화, 정신문화연구 원 박사논문, 1995

장병인, 조선중기 혼인제의 실상-반친영의 실체와 그 수용여부를 중심으로, 《역사와 현실》 58, 2005

한희숙, 양반사회와 여성의 지위, 《한국사 시민강좌》 15, 1994

전경목, 분재기(分財記)를 통해서 본 분재와 봉사(奉祀) 관행의 변천-부안 김씨 고문서를 중심으로, 《고문서연구》 22, 2003

최진순, 대동여지도와 김정호 선생의 일생, 《학생》 창간호, 1929.1.

신영철, 고산자 김정호 선생 이약이 1, 《어린이》 7권 3호, 1929

최남선, 70년 전에 단신 실사독력(實査獨力) 창제한 고산자의 대 동여지도, 《별건곤》, 1928년 5월호/ 《육당 최남선 전집》 9, 현암사, 1974 재수록

최남선, 고산자를 회(懷)함, 《동아일보》 1925년 10월 8-9일/ 《육당 최남선 전집》 10, 현암사, 1974 재수록

배우성, 18세기 관찬지도 제작과 지리 인식, 서울대 박사논문, 1996

양보경, 대동여지도를 만들기까지, 《한국사 시민강좌》 16, 일 조각, 1995

이상태, 김정호는 옥사하지 않았다, 《조선역사 바로잡기》, 가 람기획, 2000

송찬섭, 1862년 농민항쟁과 진주, 《진주농민운동의 역사적 조 명》, 역사비평사, 2003

송찬섭, 1862년 진주농민항쟁의 조직과 활동, 《한국사론》 21, 1989

하현강, 이명윤의 피무사실에 대하여, 《사학연구》 18, 1964

정석종, 홍경래의 난, 《전통시대의 민중운동》 하, 풀빛, 1981

鶴園 裕, 평안도 농민전쟁의 참가층, 《전통시대의 민중운동》 상, 풀빛, 1981

김현덕, 한국 천주교 전래의 기원설에 대한 비판연구 - 1566년부 터 1784년까지, 가톨릭대학교 대학원 석사논문, 1993

최효식, 수운 최제우의 생애와 사상, 《동학연구》 제2집, 1998

조재모,전봉희, 고종조 경복궁 중건에 관한 연구, 《대한건축학 회논문집》 16권 4호(통권138), 2000.4.

한국교회사연구소 역, 한불관계자료(1866~1867) - 병인양요, 《교회사연구》 2, 1979

젊은역사연구모임, 무능과 무지의 상징 강화도조약, 《영화처럼 읽는 한국사》, 명진출판, 1999

한철호, 제1차 수신사(1876) 김기수의 견문활동과 그 의의, 《한 국사상사학》 27, 2006

한철호, 우리나라 최초의 국기('박영효 태극기' 1882)와 통리교섭 통상사무아문 제작 국기(1994)의 원형 발견과 그 역사적 의의, 《한국독립운동사연구》 31, 2008

강재언, 봉건체제 해체기의 갑오농민전쟁, 《한국근대민족운동

사》, 돌베개, 1980

이민원, 민비 시해의 배경과 구도, 《명성황후 시해사건》, 민음
  사, 1992

서영희, 명성황후 재평가, 《역사비평》, 2002년 가을호

서영희 명성황후 연구, 《역사비평》, 2001년 겨울호

이규태, 민비의 사진, 《조선일보》 '이규태 코너' 1990.3.4.

정인경, 과학기술의 도입, 그 환희와 절망, 《우리는 지난 100년
  동안 어떻게 살았을까》 1, 역사비평사, 1998

Catalogs

《안동 정상동 일선 문씨와 이응태묘 발굴조사 보고서 - 제4회
  안동대학교박물관 특별전시회 "450년만의 외출" 도록》, 안동
  대학교박물관, 2000.2

From late Joseon to the Daehan Empire

Letters from Korean History

Volume IV

First Published 5 May 2016
Third Published 10 April 2023

Author | Park Eunbong
Translator | Ben Jackson
Illustrator | Illustration: Yi Seonhee, Map: Yu Sanghyeon

Design | Lee Seokwoon, Kim Miyeon

Published by | Cum Libro Inc. **CUM LIBRO** 책과함께
Address | 2F, Sowaso Bldg. 70, Donggyo-ro, Mapo-gu, Seoul, Korea 04022
Tel | (+82) 2-335-1982
Fax | (+82) 2-335-1316
E-mail | prpub@daum.net
Blog | blog.naver.com/prpub
Registered | 3 April 2003 No. 25100-2003-392

ISBN 979-11-86293-51-5 04740
ISBN 979-11-86293-46-1 (set)